MORE CHRIST

The True Riches of Human Experience

STEVE HARTLAUB

These studies, and many others can be found at:
www.givemechrist.com

Contents

The order of the last 6 divisions of the book are taken from Philippians 3:2.

"Beware of dogs" is represented by Vanity, countered by God's Grace.

"Beware of evil workers" is represented by Spiritual Wickedness, countered by God's Righteousness.

"Beware of the concision" is represented by Religion, countered by God's Glory

INTRODUCTION

Yea, doubtless, and I count all things but loss, for the excellency of the knowledge of Christ Jesus my Lord, for whom I have suffered the loss of all things, and do count them but dung, that I may gain Christ.

It is obvious that when we become born of the spirit of God we receive all the spirit we will ever be given, because there is no size or quantity or amount with spirit. But there *is* an amount, and size, and quantity—no matter how immeasurable—concerning how much of our mind and character and life is impregnated with the life of Christ. To gain Christ is for Christ to make another inroad into another area of our life and thinking, understanding and belief. This is how we grow, how we become more spiritual. The purpose for this book is to provide inspiration and nourishment for that growth.

Gaining Christ is a lot like learning to drive a car with a manual transmission, learning how to swim, or how to fly an airplane. There are many parts to learn, and figuring out how to do them all in sync can seem a daunting task; however, it is well worth the effort. Be patient and conscientious, and apply yourself diligently.

As the days pass and another piece after another piece falls into place, what once seemed almost insurmountable will become second nature. To have gained Christ is the greatest achievement of the human experience.

I know I could be a better Biblical researcher. I know I could present the Scriptures in a more developed, thorough fashion. The purpose for my studies and this book is not to exhaust the Scripture regarding a specific topic in order to educate and convince your mind; rather, it is to present to you revelations of the Christ within me, so that when you read you may not only have my understanding of Christ, but also that you may be carried even further, by the revealing of the Christ within you, into the heart of the Father's love for you.

Every time I read one of my studies, I see another way the same truth could have been presented, another Scripture verse(s) that could have been used to convey the same truth in an even more powerful way. So when you read what I have written and think you have a better understanding, or a better way to communicate what I have written, or a better Scripture, that is a very good thing indeed, because it means the spirit of Christ is being stirred up within you. And that is the purpose for this book; not for your mind to learn what is written, but for your heart to receive the revelation of Christ. And every time this happens, you have gained Christ.

> *And be found in him, not having my own righteousness which is of the law, but that which is through the faith of Christ; the righteousness which is from out of God by faith.*

Perhaps the most powerful feedback I have received from those who read my first book, *Give Me Christ - Revelations of the Glorified Christ* was from those who told me that the book changed the way they read the Bible, allowing them to more likely hear the voice of

God and get more powerful understanding every time they read it. I pray this second book does more of the same.

SOME NOTES

I work from the King James Version of the Bible, but I quite freely change wording and punctuation in order to better represent what God is wanting to say, as I see it. This is why I seriously recommend you have your own Bible with you as you read this book. I take seriously God's admonition in II Timothy 2:15 to apply myself as a workman of His Word. If I am in error; well, God is not done with me yet! Wherever and whenever the Scripture in this book deviates from the King James, you can just figure that it is because I have arrived at what I consider a better translation of the original text(s).

I have come to understand that truth does not live in the pages of the Bible, but only in the spirit which inhabits people's hearts. When what is written becomes a living thing in the heart, that is where and when truth abides. Therefore, I have no problem changing wording in any Biblical passage, based on my research, done in an effort to have its truth live in my heart.

Regarding capitalization (or non-capitalization) of the words "spirit" and "holy spirit," I have tried in this second book to be more consistent than the first. The Holy Spirit is God. What he gives of Himself to live within us is of His holy spirit. Unless I thought that either "spirit" or "holy spirit" was speaking specifically about God Himself, I did not capitalize the words, no matter what the King James Bible did. If you do not agree with me, feel perfectly free to capitalize (or not), depending on how you interpret and understand what is written.

All studies in this book, as well as many others, can be found at: www.givemechrist.com.

The following books are priceless to me in my research of the truth of Christ:

A Critical Lexicon and Concordance to the English and Greek New Testament, E. W. Bullinger, 1975

The Interlinear Greek-English New Testament, George Ricker Berry, 1958

The Companion Bible, Appendix 104 (Prepositions), E. W. Bullinger, 1969

I want to thank some of the people who have inspired me in my quest for Christ, each of whom bears some of the credit for the existence of this book:

Sharon, Caitlin, Joel, Kirsten, Amy, Charles, Tad, Gina, Kelsey, Kayla, Jessica, Sadie Hartlaub, Dave & Eugene Hartlaub, Erin, Ivan & Edwin Benitez, Cole Kendziora, AJ & Glenda Sue Morris, Andrew & Kelsey Van Kirk, Jan & Glenn Magiera, TJ & Holly Voelske, Chris & Rebecca Collins, Sean & Libby McCarthy, Larry Harvey, Ron & Roslyn Greer, Roger Klug, Shane Hudson, Don & Theresa Jenkins, Steve & Tracey Schmidt, Tim Genin, Kurt Fiser, John Lynn, Arne Strand, Andrew & Faith Smithback, Jim & Christina McDonald, Grace Collins.

Of such is the body of Christ; and knowing, connecting with and learning from them is a large part of my heavenly inheritance.

FOUNDATIONAL STUDIES

And now for another step or two on our spiritual journey ...

IS GOD IN CONTROL
God is not a puppeteer

God is sovereign.

God is in control.

God is all-powerful.

These statements, or phrases like them, often come right after the recounting of some negative event ... a death, tragic accident, sickness, loss of a job or something like that. I cringe when I hear them because these phrases portray God as a careless overseer of the affairs of man whose best methods of instruction seem to be to visit pain and suffering on people who love Him. At worst, they make God out to be a devilish trickster who seems to delight in testing people's faith, just to see if they really love Him.

These phrases, used of God in the context of absolute control over the world and all its people and events, are man-made and devil-inspired. They are meant by the devil to make it more difficult for us to know and trust God, and if we truly believe them, they result in a spiritual theft and weakening in our lives. As the truth makes us free, so lies encase us in a bondage of contradictive understanding.

God is not capricious or cavalier in the enforcement of His power.

He does have boundaries, and His boundaries are the limitlessness of Christ. So let us take a look at these faulty concepts regarding God's power of control, and see what the Bible has to say regarding their erroneous thinking.

"Sovereign" – "having supreme control or dominion" Often associated with the idea of independence from other authority and/or freedom of action. I have never seen this word used in the Bible.

And God blessed them (man)*, and God said unto them, Be fruitful, and multiply, and replenish the earth, and subdue it; and have dominion over the fish of the sea, and over the fowl of the air, and over every living thing that moves upon the earth. (Genesis 1:28)*

So God gave at least some of His dominion away to man. He gave away to man His "sovereignty" over the earth and all living things. Did God give it away, yet somehow in reality not give it away? Did He take it back at some later date? Or rather, in the giving it away, did God truly limit Himself?

For the gifts and the calling of God are without repentance. (Romans 11:29)

The word "repentance" literally means "afterthought, a thinking after the fact" It can carry with it the meaning of changing one's mind and/or attitude concerning something after the fact, or of having regret, but not necessarily. Once God does a thing, He doesn't go back and rethink about it afterward, and He certainly doesn't change His mind or attitude about it, or feel bad about it.

And it repented the Lord that He had made man on the earth, and it grieved Him at His heart. And the Lord said,

I will destroy man whom I have created from the face of the earth; both man, and beast, and the creeping thing, and the fowls of the air; for it repents Me that I have made them. (Genesis 6:6, 7)

If you take what these verses are saying at face value, then you must reject what is told us in Romans 11:29. And this is what many people do, and because they do, their view of God is of a capricious, vindictive, ever-changing God who rules however He happens to feel at the time. "Today, I like you, but don't piss Me off, or I'll wipe you out." What's more, the Old Testament seems to support this capricious view of God. In fact, God in the Old Testament seems very different from the God of the New Testament, who was perfectly displayed in the very non-violent, always-loving life of His son Jesus. Yes, it seems that from Old Testament to New, God did change. Yet according to God, He does not change.

For I am the Lord, I change not; therefore you sons of Jacob are not consumed. (Malachi 3:6)

Since God doesn't change, then it must be man's ability to understand God which has changed. In the New Testament, man (in whom the spirit of Christ dwells) has been born of God's holy spirit (His very nature) and therefore has the inherent ability to know the true God, as well as to discern the devil and and his workings. Old Testament man had neither of these abilities.

In the Old Testament, man could not come into harmony with God, because his very nature was contrary, out of harmony, with God's nature. Once you become born of the spirit of the risen Christ, you are an entirely different creation than any and every person mentioned in the Old Testament, with the exception of Jesus himself. (We even have it better than Jesus did when he walked the earth, in that we are not under the law).

Verily I say unto you, Among them that are born of women

> *there has not risen a greater* (one) *than John the Baptist;*
> *notwithstanding he that is least in the kingdom of heaven is*
> *greater than he. (Matthew 11:11)*

Some say God "has a plan," meaning that everything which happens falls into that plan. Is that true? Definitely not! God does have a plan, but that plan only takes place in and through and by means of Jesus Christ.

> *According to the purpose of the ages, which He purposed in*
> *Christ Jesus our Lord. (Ephesians 3:11)*

> *That in the administration of the fullness of times He might*
> *gather together in one all things in Christ, both which are*
> *in heaven and which are on earth; even in him* (Christ)*;*
> *(Ephesians 1:10)*

You see, if I wack my head and get a concussion, that's not a part of God's plan. Nor if Uncle Fred dies is that a part of God's plan. Now if Uncle Joe believes unto Jesus Christ at Uncle Fred's funeral, his believing *is* a part of God's plan!

> *Forasmuch then as the children are partakers of flesh and blood,*
> *he also himself likewise took part of the same; that through*
> *death he might destroy him who had the power of death; that*
> *is, the devil; And deliver them who through fear of death were*
> *all their lifetime subject to bondage. (Hebrews 2:14, 15)*

The devil is not the agent of God, sent to carry out God's will, neither can God contradict Himself. It is impossible for God to kill, because He sent His son Jesus Christ to die in order to defeat death and the one who wields it, the devil. Can you see how believing that God kills, or maims and injures, will make it very difficult to learn to trust Him, or to even make any sense of His Word?

Who (God) *will have all men be saved, and to come unto the knowledge* (epignosis - intimate experiential knowing) *of the truth. (I Timothy 2:4)*

God wants all men to be saved. Are all men saved? No. Will all men be saved? According to the book of Revelation, no. Then that means God's will doesn't always happen. That is absolutely correct. God's will does not always come to pass ... except in Christ Jesus our Lord.

For all the promises of God in him (Christ) *are yea, and in him Amen, unto the glory of God by us. (II Corinthians 1:20)*

"In Control" - "to have free use of directive power and authority." If God has the power and authority to freely direct his creation, then why is there so much chaos? If God can simply control man, why does He entreat man, encourage him, explain, command, instruct him? These are not the actions of one who can simply control behavior and circumstances.

In His Word, especially the Pauline epistles, God explains to us how His life works within us; how to walk in, and the benefit of walking in, that life. If He simply controlled us, there would be no need for any of this explanation or instruction.

A puppeteer directs the actions of his puppets, he is in control of them. He does not encourage them to do what he wants, he *makes* them do what he wants. Is God in control of us? Is He in control of all events and situations? If He were, then He would be evil, at least in part, because evil is happening in the world all the time.

"All-powerful" - the greatest power. If you ask 10 Christians what this expression means, you'll get 10 different explanations. The above is my explanation. There is no greater power than God's. However, God's power is not always "in play," is not always in free operation, for He has truly limited Himself as regards man. He gave dominion to man; and as it was man who lost, or gave up that dominion, so it was man who had to reacquire it.

> *For if by one man's offense death reigned by one; much more they who receive abundance of grace and of the gift of righteousness shall reign in life by one, Jesus Christ. For as by one man's disobedience many were made sinners, so by the obedience of one* (man) *shall many be made righteous. (Romans 5:17, 19)*

> *And* (you, God) *have given him* (me, Jesus) *authority to execute judgment also, because he is the son of man. (John 5:27)*

Yes it was God's will that no one ever sin, and it was God's will that all men be saved by the work of Jesus Christ, who lived and died by the will of God. But in all His will, God never ever took control and made anyone do anything. Jesus, the son of God, knew how his Father worked.

> *And he went a little further, and fell on his face, and prayed, saying, O my Father, if it be possible, let this cup pass from me; nevertheless not as I will, but as You will. (Matthew 26:39)*

In all his lifetime on earth, Jesus never once prayed, "O God, take control." He never once proclaimed that His Father was sovereign, or all-powerful, or in control. He came to carry out the will of his Father, because God could not do it without him.

> *Jesus said on them, My meat is to do the will of Him who sent me, and to finish His work. (John 4:34)*

So do not ever think that when evil happens, that God somehow caused it to happen "for a good reason." Do not think that God's will shall come to pass simply because God is "in control," or because He is "all-powerful."

There's a poem which starts like this: "God has no hands but our hands with which to give them bread; He has no feet but our feet with which to walk among the almost dead." May God's good will continue to come to pass in and through and by means of the lives of those who allow the spirit of the risen Christ to direct their hearts and lives, now and forever.

And be not conformed to this world, but be transformed by the renewing of your mind, that you may prove (in your life) *what is that good and acceptable and perfect will of God. (Romans 12:2)*

WORK VS RESULTS

You can not produce Godly results by your own ability

One big cause of stress, anxiety, bondage and sickness among Christians is confusion between the work we are to do versus the results we are to get. By wasting time focusing on the results or lack thereof, instead of focusing on the work itself, we set ourselves up for stress, worry, headaches and heartaches of all kinds.

The world teaches man that he is responsible for the results he is to obtain: Success in life, including lots of money, a rewarding, prestigious job, successful marriage, dynamic family, respectability, etc. But this is impossible as it regards the things of God, simply because we are not God.

> *Therefore take no thought* (don't be full of stress and anxiety)*; saying, What shall we eat? or, What shall we drink? or With what shall we be clothed? (For after all these things do the Gentiles seek:) for your heavenly Father knows that you have need of all these things. But seek first the kingdom of God, and His righteousness; and all these things shall be added unto you. Take therefore no thought* (don't be full of stress and anxiety about) *for tomorrow; for tomorrow shall take thought* (be full of stress and anxiety about) *for the things of itself. Sufficient*

unto the day is the evil thereof. (Matthew 6:31-33)

When you decide that you'd like to grow your own apples, you never become responsible for producing the fruit. Perhaps you get a book about how to grow apple trees, or look up that information online, and then you do what you can do to the best of your ability; buying seeds, planting them in the best way you know how in good soil, keeping them and the plant which springs up watered and fertilized; but you leave the growing of the tree up to God.

If I were to become responsible for producing the apples, what might it look like? I'd dig a hole, stick a big pole or 2x4 in the hole and refill it with dirt. There, now I have a piece of wood to which I can attach other pieces of wood and then apples. So I screw, nail and staple pieces of wood at all angles to that piece of wood sticking out of the ground, and finally I staple apples all around and voila! the best results I can obtain by my own efforts! God didn't directly have a thing to do with it!

It seems a foolish analogy, but this is exactly why there is so much stress and worry and anxiety and bondage and sickness in people's lives ... they are trying to obtain the results that only God can produce. In the above verse, God sets us straight. Let anxiety about tomorrow be tomorrow's anxiety (and tomorrow never comes!). You do what you can do in seeking The One who can produce good results, and leave the actual results up to God.

I understand this is an alien way of thinking to the western mind, but this is the life God has called us to; therefore, it must be possible to be lived!

Here's another analogy. Let's say I'm a carpenter, and I decide I want to build a home for my best friend and his family because I love them so much. I want them to have a home of their own where they can raise happy, healthy kids and grow old together. I can build the house, but by no effort of my own can I produce that happy, healthy family.

> *I have planted, Apollos watered; but God gave the increase.*
> *(I Corinthians 3:6)*

So one day you're sitting in a church service, and the preacher is teaching about how we need to become more loving, or more peaceful, or joyful, or more kind. Ever heard a teaching like that? What that well-intentioned preacher is teaching is that we should be trying to obtain, by our own efforts, the results that only God can produce in our lives. Is it any wonder so many Christians live defeated lives? They're ignoring the work they *can* do in favor of trying to produce the results that they *can in no way* do!

> *But the fruit of the Spirit is love, joy, peace, longsuffering, gentleness, goodness, faith, Meekness, temperance; regarding such things there is no law. (Galatians 5:22, 23)*

There is no effort which would be required by any law, rule, principle or guideline that can produce any of this fruit in our lives. Only the spirit of God can produce this fruit. So where is our effort to be directed? Why, into walking by the spirit that produces the fruit, of course! And "to walk by" means to walk in. We walk in the spirit of God, meaning wherever that spirit goes, we go with it. In order to stay in it, we have to go where it goes, believe what it teaches us, follow the "laws" it writes in our hearts. (We can not depart from it simply because our Pastor is telling us something different). The result of walking in the spirit of God is the fruit specified above!

How would you like to be more steady and focused in your life? Wiser? Hear more often from God? Know God's heart more? Become more understanding of the why's and wherefore's of life? Become clearer on God's expectations of and for you? Know what you're going to be able to do before you're able to do it? Grow more able to handle whatever comes your way? More victorious over all your life's challenges and problems? How would you like to feel like there is no limit to what is possible for your life? Nothing too big to overcome, no Godly desire that can not be achieved?

Stop trying to get the results, and focus on the effort or work that is required of you!

> *Wherefore I also, after I heard of your believing in the Lord Jesus and love unto all the saints* (you are walking in that which has been given you, sharing it with others), *Cease not to give thanks for you, making mention of you in my prayers: That the God of our Lord Jesus Christ, the Father of glory, may give unto you the spirit of wisdom and revelation in the intimate knowing (epignosis) of him; the eyes of your understanding being enlightened; that you may know what is the hope of His calling, and what* (is) *the riches of the glory of his inheritance in the saints, And what is the exceeding greatness of His power toward us who believe ... (Ephesians 1:15-19a)*

Understand clearly what work you can do, staying clear of trying to produce the results in your life that only God can produce. In the above verses, the work a man can do is to walk in the faith that he has, seeing its benefits in more and more areas of his life, and then becoming more willing to share what he has of value with others. That is the work you can do. The rest of what is described in the above verses is up to God.

> *For it is God who works in you both to will and to do of His good pleasure. (Philippians 2:13)*

Does this sound like God wants you to produce spiritual results in your own life? By your own efforts? No! God gives something to you. Now you 1) enjoy it; and 2) share it with others. Now God gives you more. Now you 1) enjoy it; and 2) share it with others. Now God gives you more. Now you ... well, you get the picture.

Until you enjoy (use, are influenced by, walk in the truth of, are thankful for) what God has given you, and then share what is in you of God with others, as His spirit leads, there will be little to no spiritual fruit being produced in your life.

I was once speaking to a full time minister, who felt that it was the will of God for his ministry to spread to China, but that it was not God's will that he himself go; rather, that someone involved in his ministry should go. The time was fast approaching where a decision would have to be made as to who would go as a representative of this man's ministry, yet he had not been able to find the right person, and this was causing a lot of stress in his life and thinking. I looked him in the eyes and said, "If it is God's idea that someone else go, then wouldn't it be God's responsibility to supply that someone? Why are you acting like the burden is on your shoulders to get the results God has said He wants?" And then I quoted the above verse from Philippians. He was "stopped in his tracks" as he looked at me, and all the stress and burden just melted away (it was a beautiful thing to see), and he exclaimed, "Of course, it's up to God to bring to pass His will for my life!"

> *Let us labor therefore to enter into that rest, lest any man fall after the same example of unbelief.* (the example of Israel, who would not enter into the Promised Land originally because they did not believe God would give it to them without their own efforts, resulting in them being a nomadic tribe for 40 years). *(Hebrews 4:11)*

This verse talks about us working. But is it the effort to produce the results of rest? No.

> *For he that is entered into His rest, he also has ceased from his own works, as God did from His. (Hebrews 4:10)*

The labor God requires of us is the effort to stop trying to achieve the results which only He, God, can produce in our lives.

Let us therefore fear, lest, a promise being left us of entering into His rest, any of you should seem to come short of it. For unto us was the gospel preached, as well as unto them; but the word preached did not profit them, not being mixed with faith in them that heard it. (Hebrews 4:1, 2)

The labor God requires of us is the effort to accept by believing what God has promised (by revelation) we shall have. It is up to us to receive it, enjoy it and share its benefit with others.

So what has God promised you? I'm not speaking generally here. Specifically, what has God promised you? What has He told you, by the revelation of the spirit of His son within you, that He has done for you, given you, worked in you, given you the ability to do? What Has He promised you He will do for you, give you, provide for you? I encourage you to simply accept what He has promised you as being an accomplished work in and for your life. And then, as you start seeing its fulfillment in your life, share the benefit you receive with others. Leave the rest up to God.

And God is able to make all grace abound toward you; that you, always having all sufficiency in all things, may abound to every good work; Now He that ministers seed to the sower both minister bread for your food, and multiply your seed sown, and increase the fruits of your righteousness;Being enriched in every thing to all bountifulness, which causes through us thanksgiving to God. (II Corinthians 9:8, 10, 11)

GOD'S POINT OF VIEW

God's point of view is Christ

Man-as-god tends to think that he is capable of arriving at truth - at objective truth - by his own mental endeavoring. But does such a thing as "objective truth" even exist? I believe that all understanding is subjective; that is, it is colored by the perception of the one doing the understanding. Therefore, if "objective truth" does exist, it is impossible for man to have it in his understanding without it becoming subjective. No, the thing to strive for is not "objective truth," which is colored by the perception of each man; but rather to arrive at God's perception of truth, which can only be received and understood by the working of God's spirit within us, also known as "the mind of Christ."

> *For my thoughts are not your thoughts, neither are your ways my ways, says the Lord. For as the heavens are higher than the earth, so are My ways higher than your ways, and my thoughts than your thoughts. (Isaiah 55:8, 9)*

The above was true in the Old Testament, when no man could think the thoughts of the spirit, when no man could see into the kingdom of God. Jesus Christ has made possible the God-like ability to think like God thinks, to actually have His point of view!

Freedom, fulfillment, dynamic inner strength, fruitful purpose; all these are possible through the reality of the spirit of the glorified Christ. They are not possible within the realm of the mind which deals with life from a fixed perspective of emotional and fleshly understanding and decision making. Rather, they are only possible where "I" live in the presence of God's point of view, which is Christ.

God's point of view is truth. Truth is how creation is designed to work. God's point of view is how things are designed to work, because those things were created by His point of view!

The Word of God is that which God communicates, or expresses. Another way of understanding this "logos" of God is: God expressing His point of view.

> *In the beginning was the word, and the word was with God, and the word was God. The same was in the beginning with God. All things were made by it, and without it was not made anything that was made. In it was life, and the life was the light of men. (John 1:1-4)*

A lot of people simply gloss over these verses in the gospel of John, thinking that this "word" means Jesus, but that is a disservice to the truth these verses convey. Rather, God is telling us that the expression of His point of view carries the life-giving power of His creative ability. In verse 14, "And the word was made flesh and dwelt among us ...", this is telling us that God's creative life-giving point of view became embodied in the man Jesus, the Christ.

Opinion, moral judgment, behavior modification ... these do not exist in the realm of the truth of God's point of view. What does exist in God's point of view is a spiritually loving creative intent to bring God's own being into full blown (glorious) expression, and He has invited man into the ability to conscientiously partake of this expression!

For the invisible things of Him from the creation of the world are clearly seen, being understood by the things that are made … His eternal power and deity, so that they (man) *are without excuse. (Romans 1:20)*

God's point of view is totally subjective, and He desires that man be like-mindedly subjective; that is, to "see" things like He does.

*Be you therefore followers (*mimetes* - mimics, or imitators) of God, as dear children; (Ephesians 5:1)*

But how can a man, by his own mind, think like God, who is most definitely not a man, but rather is spirit (John 4:24)? The only way to do this, of course, is by means of the gift of the mind of Christ.

… But we have the mind of Christ. (I Corinthians 2:16b)

And because we have the mind of Christ, we can think, or have the exact same point of view, as Christ, which is God's point of view! Too often, "we should be more like Christ" is interpreted to mean acting like Christ acted. But that cannot be the case. (Change water to wine, walk on water, die on the cross.....!!) What allows us to be like Christ is not only having his powerful life within us, but also having the ability to think like he thought, to feel what he felt, to have his exact point of view.

Let this mind be in you, which was also in Christ Jesus; Who, being in the form of God, thought … (Philippians 2:5ff)

Again, many people focus on the phrase "Who, being in the form of God" as meaning that Jesus is God. And again, this is a disservice to the wonderful truth of this word, which is telling us to think with the same mind as Christ, to have his exact point of view. And when you read the verses which follow Philippians 2:5, you will see that we also, being begotten as God's children in His image (form), are able to think exactly what Christ thought, because we have the mind of his spiritual point of view!

> *And He* (God) *that searches the hearts knows what is the mind* (the thinking) *of the spirit, because it* (the spirit) *makes intercession for the saints according to God. (Romans 8:27)*

He not only asks us to view life and creation like He does, He also gives us the ability to do so!

> *For it God who works* (energizes) *within you both to will and to do of His good pleasure. (Philippians 2:13)*

This ability does not spring from our minds that we have had and used for thinking since our physical birth. Rather, it springs from the mind (ability to think) of Christ, which was created within us when we first believed unto Jesus Christ.

> *Therefore if any man be in Christ, he is a new creation; old things are passed away; behold, all things are become new. And all things* (new) *are of God … (II Corinthians 5:17, 18a)*

> *And that you put on the new man, which after* (resourced from) *God is created in righteousness and true holiness. (Ephesians 4:24)*

God doesn't see things as they are, but rather as they are intended to become. God's point of view is always a "becoming." He sees creation as a continual flowering, growing, developing, improving,

> *Of His own will He begat us* (brought us forth) *by the word of truth* (by the expression of His point of view!)*, that we should be a kind of firstfruits of his created beings. (James 1:18)*

I've heard it said that to "create" means to make something from nothing; but in truth, creation is the spiritual being expressed in the physical world.

> *While we look not at the things which are seen, but at the*

things which are not seen; for the things which are seen are
temporal; but the things which are not seen are eternal.
(II Corinthians 4:18)

This describes God's point of view. And He is continually inviting us to have the same point of view … the view of the eternal, of the invisible. Where all is of God; where fullness and fruitful growth and development are the truth, where all things are unto the praise of His full and complete self-expression.

And be not conformed (shaped) *to this world, but be transformed*
by the renewing of your mind, in order that you may prove (see
successfully in action) *what is that good and acceptable and*
perfect will of God. (Romans 12:2)

That we should be to praise of His glory (full expression), *who*
first trusted in Christ. (Ephesians 1:12)

THE BENEFITS OF TRIBULATION

It is at the point of attack where real growth occurs

The point of this study is to arrive at an outlook concerning our mental and emotional struggles which best positions us for spiritual growth and a closer relationship with God, our Father. Most view these kind of struggles as a negative thing, something to be avoided. After digesting the truth of the content of this study, my prayer is that you become more thankful and hopeful wherever and whenever you encounter strong mental, emotional, psychological resistance to your well-being.

For it is at the very point of the attack, at that place in our hearts and minds where the trials or tribulations of life are making their greatest impact, that the potential for growth and empowerment is at its greatest. Without this struggle there can be no growth. The strongest people are those who push against the biggest weights.

And when they (Paul and Barnabas) *had preached the gospel to that city* (Derbe) *and had taught many; they returned again to Lystra and Iconium, and Antioch, Confirming the souls of the disciples, and exhorting them to continue in the faith, and that we must through much tribulation enter into the kingdom of God. (Acts 14:21, 22)*

Remember that the kingdom of God is the spiritual realm where God's will dominates.

> *For the kingdom of God is not meat and drink; but righteousness, and peace, and joy in the holy spirit. (Romans 14:17)*

The word "tribulation" is the Greek word *thlipsis* and is translated "tribulation," "affliction" and "trouble." Its root word is *thlibo* and is primarily translated "afflict" or "trouble," but its first use is very illuminating.

> *Because strait is the gate, and narrow (thlibo) is the way, which leads unto life, and few there be that find it. (Matthew 7:14)*

The word "strait" in this verse means "narrow," and the word "narrow" *(thlibo)* could be better translated "compressed." Like a challenging mountain trail which grows narrower as it nears the summit, but is the only way to the top of the mountain, you can't simply veer off it and expect to safely reach the top; and even though there might be drop-offs on one side, and the face of a cliff on the other, leaving you without much extra room, it's the only way to the top. So God tells us that it is only by means of a journey which presses or squeezes us that we can enter into the kingdom of God.

Why? Because we walk in our old ways until and unless we come to the point where our old ways will simply not work anymore, and it is at that very point where spiritual breakthroughs occur. At the point where the old man is confronted by the fruitlessness of his endeavors, where nothing in his arsenal can overcome the present foe; it is at that very point that the way and will of God, being urgently required, comes into its glory (full expression) in our minds and hearts and lives. It is by being thus squeezed that we grow spiritually and manifest forth our spiritual citizenship.

And not only so, but we glory in tribulations also; knowing that tribulation works patience; And patience, experience; and experience, hope; And hope makes not ashamed ...(Romans 5:3-5a)

The word in the King James "works" is better translated "works out," like you work out your strength, your muscles, your endurance when you go to the gym. So tribulation gets our patience going, which gets our experience (*gnosis* - relational experience of God) going, which gets our hope going. In other words, what helps bring that which we spiritually hope for into the realm of reality in our lives is ultimately tribulation. And that is why we glory in it.

To use the image of working out at the gym, imagine being out of shape and starting your journey of physical improvement. First, you sign up (believe unto Jesus Christ), then you do your first workout (tribulation). You can't do much, sweating is sure a novelty, and it hurts so much (especially over the next week or so); yet you experience little or no physical improvement. Ahh! You need patience! So you take on a new mindset. You realize that this journey is not going to happen all at once, so you settle in, learning to "enjoy the suck" as they say (glory in tribulation). You learn to enjoy the physical discomfort and exertion, patiently waiting for the growth. And so you begin to experience real gains in your strength and endurance, becoming stronger in very measurable increments. And as that happens, the expectations (hope) which initiated this journey, becoming reality, are thus justified (no shame).

At the point of attack, where the fruitlessness of the sinful man is coming up against the call to victory of the spirit of Christ, that's where real breakthrough into God's kingdom occurs; where our identity changes from carnal to spiritual, where vanity is replaced by thankfulness for the spiritual gifts received, weakness is replaced by spiritual strength and confidence, selfishness is replaced by love, and darkness is replaced by wisdom and spiritual understanding.

Victories occur at the points of attack.

It is our flesh which is squeezed, not the spirit of Christ.

> *These things I have spoken unto you, that in me you might have peace. In the world you shall have tribulation; but be of good cheer; I have overcome the world. (John 16:33)*

Are you becoming aware of your inability to really love your wife and children amidst all your selfishness and sin? Praise the Lord! Go to the well of Christ and see what strength, what wisdom, what understanding he can supply you with. Are you tired of being beaten down by your fear and depression? Know that it is where you feel Satan's attacks the strongest that the victory of Christ in your life will be greatest. Are you frustrated continually by your giving in to anger and arguing? Lay that frustration down at the foot of the cross and expect to see God raise up a new man in you which is completely unaffected by what used to anger and consume you.

Our spiritual growth occurs little by little, with an occasional leap in growth. It is simply not an "all or none" thing like many Christian churches teach. At those specific times and places where you feel your weakest, it is there, right there in that psychological, mental, emotional squeezing, that you finally give up your old way and reach forth unto the high calling of God in Christ Jesus, where you confront Satan's afflictions which have dominated you for so long, where you grow to become like spiritual teflon to his attacks. It is in that pressure where you refuse to go back to your old way, instead demanding of God that what He has promised for you become yours in practice and in reality in your life. And that is when it happens, when and where it needs to happen!

So at your next point of attack, where the squeezing of the trials and temptations of the old man are meeting the promises and calling of the spirit of Christ, be gloriously thankful, because such a squeezing can only occur because you have been called to something greater, and you will never again be satisfied or content by the world's offerings. That hope which sprang up in you and turned you away from your own lack when you first believed, will continue to bring the experience of God into your heart and life as you patiently endure the sinful man being squeezed out of you once and for all.

> *And he* (the Lord) *said unto me, My grace is sufficient for you; for my strength is made perfect in* (your) *weakness. Most gladly therefore will I rather glory in my infirmities* (weaknesses), *that the power of Christ may rest upon me. Therefore I take pleasure in infirmities, in reproaches* (shame, dishonor), *in necessities, in persecutions, in distresses for the sake of Christ; for when I am weak, then am I strong. (II Corinthians 12:9, 10)*

THE CHRIST

Get him – so that you have him - and you've got it all

THE NAMES—JESUS, CHRIST AND LORD

Let's take a look at each of these names, titles, appellations, designations. We'll look at what and who they meant, what and who they mean now. Does Jesus live in us? Does the term "Christ in you" mean another human being is living inside you? Is the Lord of the Old Testament the same as the Lord of the New?

LORD

The word "Lord" indicates one having rightful authority over another. In most of today's cultures, a common word that has a similar meaning would be "boss." The one referred to as "Lord" in the Old Testament is not the one referred to as "Lord" in the New Testament (except in those cases where the New Testament is referencing the Old). Jesus was not Lord in the Old Testament.

The first time God refers to Himself as Lord is Genesis 2:4. The word is specifically used in the context of His relationship with man.

> *These are the generations of the heavens and of the earth when they were created, in the day that the Lord God made the earth and the heavens. And the Lord God formed man of the dust of the ground, and breathed into his nostrils the breath of life; and*

man became a living soul. And the Lord God planted a garden eastward in Eden; and there He put the man whom He had formed. (Genesis 2:4, 7, 8)

Lord means boss, and before God created man in His image, He was creator, but not boss. The name "lord" indicates a give and take relationship (the lord exercises authority, the subject dutifully responds), which God never had until He had made man in His image (His image is spirit - John 4:24). Before man, all of creation simply operated according to the "foundation" God had supplied His creation.

According as He has chosen us in him (Christ) before the foundation of the world (kosmos) that we should be holy and without blame before Him in love. (Ephesians 1:4)

When the Creator made man in His image, placing within man His spirit; His relationship with that man was something new, as far as we know. He became Lord. Thus He worked with man, having given him the ability to act independently.

And the Lord God took the man, and put him into the garden of Eden to dress it and to keep it. And the Lord God commanded the man, saying, Of every tree of the garden you may freely eat; But of the tree of the knowledge of good and evil, you shall not eat of it; for in the day that you eat thereof you shall surely die. (Genesis 2:15, 16)

Some people believe God put the tree of the knowledge of good and evil in the garden so that man would have a choice. Some even believe God did so to test whether man would love and obey Him or not. Crazy ideas! Man had plenty of choices available to him. What to name the animals, what to name his children, when and how to make love with Eve; what to do that day, what to eat, where to go. Are these not choices? Why does choice mean a choice between good and evil? Because Adam and Eve ate of that tree, that's why. They shouldn't have; life would have stayed simple and beautiful and all good. Instead, here's what happened:

> *Because that which may be known of God is manifest in them; for God has showed it unto them. For the invisible things of Him from the creation of the world are clearly seen, being understood by the things that are made; His eternal power and deity* (God-ness); *so that they are without excuse; Because that, when they knew God, they glorified Him not as God, neither were thankful; but became vain in their imaginations* (due to eating of the tree of the knowledge of good and evil), *and their foolish heart was darkened. Professing themselves to be wise, they became fools. (Romans 1:19-22)*

Throughout the Old Testament, the Creator is in the position of Lord to man. He dealt with man as Lord through intermediaries (prophets, angels, in dreams, etc., even a burning bush!) because after man lost the spirit of God, he had no way to deal directly with his Lord, God. That changes in the New Testament.

> *Therefore let all the house of Israel know assuredly, that God has made that same Jesus, whom you have crucified, both Lord and Christ. (Acts 2:36)*

The point at which God the Creator handed the mantel of His Lordship over to Jesus is specified in Ephesians.

> *And what is the exceeding greatness of His power toward us who believe, according to the working of His mighty power, Which He worked in Christ, when He raised him from the dead, and set him at His own right hand in the heavenlies* (the spiritual realm), *Far above every principality, and authority, and might, and lordship, and every name that is named, not only in this age, but also in that which is to come; And has put all things under his feet, and gave him to be the head over all things for the church, Which is his body, the fullness of him*

who fills all in all. (Ephesians 1:19-23)

When God seated Jesus as the Christ at His right hand, that is the point at which Jesus was made Lord over all. The fullness of this lordship will not come about until the period of time spoken of in the book of Revelation, which begins after the gathering together of the saints. Until then, Jesus' lordship is exercised within and toward his body, the church, by means of the working of the holy spirit of God. The "body" of this finishing work of the holy spirit of God within man is known as "Christ."

Now the Lord is that spirit, and where the spirit of the Lord is, there is liberty. (II Corinthians 3:17)

CHRIST

"Christ" means "the anointing" or "the anointed one." The Old Testament word is "messiah" *(maschiach)*. An anointing by God indicated the promised and purposeful presence and working of God toward man. The first time this word was used in the Old Testament is in Genesis:

God speaking to Jacob: *I am the God of Bethel, where you anointed the pillar* (of rock), *and where you vowed a vow unto me: (Genesis 31:13a)*

Jacob had built a little pile (pillar) of stones, and poured oil on it, in memory of what God had promised him, which was:

And he dreamed, and behold a ladder set up on the earth, and the top of it reached to heaven; and behold the angels of God ascending and descending on it. And behold, the Lord stood above it, and said, I am the Lord God of Abraham your father, and the God of Isaac; the land whereon you lie, to you will I give it, and to your seed; and your seed shall be as the dust of the earth, and you shall spread abroad to the west, and to the

> *east, and to the north, and to the south: and in you and in your*
> *seed shall all the families of the earth be blessed. And behold, I*
> *am with you, and will keep you in all places where you go,*
> *and will bring you again into this land; for I will not leave*
> *you until I have done that which I have spoken to you of.*
> *(Genesis 28:12-15)*

The anointing, then, represented to Jacob what God had promised to Jacob at that time, which was: 1) free and unlimited access to heaven, the spiritual realm; 2) ownership and dominion of the land where he and his seed lived and would ever live; 3) an ever-increasing fruitfulness of offspring; and 4) the continual and unending presence, protection and blessing of God.

All of the above are brought to pass in Christ.

> *The spirit of the Lord* (God) *is upon me, because He has*
> *anointed* (christ-ified) *me to preach the gospel to the poor* (in
> spirit)*; He has sent me to heal the brokenhearted, to preach*
> *deliverance to the captives, and recovering of* (spiritual) *sight*
> *to the blind, to send forth in deliverance the broken down, To*
> *preach the acceptable year of the Lord. (Luke 4:18, 19)*

It was after being baptized by John, immediately after which the spiritual realm was opened unto him and his Father testified of His pleasure in His son, and then after that the tempting in the wilderness for 40 days, during which his obedience to his Father was proven, that Jesus was made the Christ, at the very place he had been raised to adulthood. It was then and there that Jesus became the anointed one of God, the Christ, and it was done by "the spirit of the Lord."

> *And he closed the book, and he gave it again to the minister, and*
> *sat down. And the eyes of all them that were in the synagogue*
> *were fastened on him. And he began to say unto them, This day*
> *is this scripture fulfilled in your ears. (Luke 4:20, 21)*

This anointing represented the four attributes I listed above: 1) free spiritual access; 2) re-established dominion over the earth; 3) ever-increasing fruitfulness; and 4) eternal protection, blessing and presence of God. And these four attributes are established by Christ as realities in this world, by means of that same "spirit of the Lord" which made Jesus the Christ.

Lest you think that Christ and the holy spirit are two different spirits, please take a look at Ephesians 4.

> *There is one body, and one spirit, even as you are called in one hope of your calling; One Lord, one faith, one baptism, One God and Father of all, who is above all, and through all, and in you all. (Ephesians 4:4-6)*

There is one spirit. You can not say there are two. If you say "One Lord" means there is another, then I will say that "One God and Father" (Who is "in you all") means there are three spirits (or even four!) in man, and that is foolishness, because Ephesians 4:4 says there is only one spirit. The one spirit which dwells within us is from out of the Father, God. He dwells within us by means of His holy spirit, also referred to as Christ. This "Christ" is the same spirit with which God the Father anointed His son. These different names for the one spirit within us are simply different facets of that one spirit. I am a father, brother, son, boss, friend and husband, but I am not 6 different people; rather, I relate to people in those 6 different ways (among others).

So today the term "Christ" does not so much reference a man (though it can, and the context always makes that perfectly clear), but rather the culminating working of God which began in Jesus and now continues in those who have believed unto his name. Christ is the working of God which will (re) establish all His original and true desire toward man-in-His-image. You can see these exact attributes of His original desire established toward man in Genesis:

> *So God created man in His image, in the image of God created He him* (free and unlimited spiritual access); *male and female created He them. And God blessed them* (the blessing of God), *and God said unto them, Be fruitful, and multiply, and fill the earth* (fruitfulness of offspring), *and subdue it; and have dominion* (dominion) *over the fish of the sea, and over the fowl of the air, and over every living thing that moves upon the earth. (Genesis 1:27, 28)*

When the Bible speaks of "Christ in you," it's not talking about a man in us, but rather the finishing work of God's holy spirit (sanctifying spirit) within us, working to re-establish this original desire of God for and toward man. This re-establishing of God's original desire in man is already a completed work in Jesus, making him *the* Christ. That completed work is what is presently at work within the group of those who have accepted the lordship of Jesus as the Christ. Thus is it also known as "Christ in you (plural)."

> *But you have an anointing from the holy One* (Jesus), *and you know all things* (of the spirit, whatever the anointing has revealed within). *But the anointing which you have received of him abides in you, and you need not that any man teach you; but as the same anointing teaches you of all things, and is truth, and is no lie, and even as it has taught you, you shall abide in it. (I John 2:20, 27)*

We know of God and of heavenly things only what the spirit of God within, the anointing, Christ, reveals within us. We can only walk in the reality of the spirit as and to the degree the spirit reveals itself within. Besides giving us the life of God, the spirit's primary purpose is to reveal the Christ within us, the completed work of God.

> *To whom God would make known what is the riches of the*

glory of this mystery among the Gentiles; which is Christ in you, the hope of glory. (Colossians 1:27)

JESUS

Jesus was (and is) a man. He was and is "the son of man," the physically born being and the means by which God would bring about the necessary judgment of His creation, as well as the re-establishment of His original spiritual intent.

> *For as the Father has life in Himself; so has He given to the son to have life in himself; And has given him authority to execute judgment also, because he is the son of man. Marvel not at this; for the hour is coming, in the which all that are in the graves shall hear his voice. And shall come forth; they who have done good, unto the resurrection of life; and they who have done evil, unto the resurrection of damnation. (John 5:26-29)*

Jesus, as a man, chose to believe and obey all his Father told him.

> *For there is one God, and one mediator between God and men, the man Christ* (anointed)*, Jesus; (I Timothy 2:5)*

"Christ' was not Jesus' last name. He was actually known as "Jesus of Nazareth," and for further delineation from others as "son of Joseph." Whenever the Bible refers to Jesus as "Christ," it is referring to his anointing by the spirit of God to the task of re-establishing the original and true purpose of God toward man.

"Christ in you" is that same anointing of the holy spirit of God within you. That Christ in you is a "person" only to the degree that it first belonged to Jesus, who freely shares it with the world, to be received by anyone who chooses to believe unto him, Jesus, as being the Christ. It is then powerfully manifested through those lives which have received it by means of a continuous subjection to Jesus' lordship, which is a spiritual lordship.

> *Howbeit when he, the spirit of truth, is come, he will guide you into all truth; for he shall not speak of himself; but whatsoever he shall hear* (from me), *that shall he speak; and he will show you things to come* (which will be true when the spirit comes). *He shall glorify me; for he shall receive of mine, and shall show it unto you. All things that the Father has are mine; therefore said I that he shall take of mine, and shall show it unto you. (John 16:13-15)*

Jesus is the man, born of a woman. As a man, Jesus was guided by the anointing spirit of God (making him the Anointed One - Christ) to re-establish God's original and true intent for man and all His creation. Jesus exercised his free will in always choosing to obey his Father, God. As a man, he became obedient unto the death of the cross, and was raised from the dead and seated at the right hand of God (position of authority and power), making him Lord over all creation. As Lord, he has sent this same anointing spirit (Christ) into the world to be received as a gift by those who accept it, and to be a benefit to those who continue to choose to walk in it.

> *But when the Comforter is come, whom I will send unto you from* (my spiritual position) *beside the Father, even the spirit of truth, which proceeds from* (me, in my spiritual position) *beside the Father, it shall testify of me. (John 15:26)*

IN THE NAME OF JESUS

In the name belonging to Jesus

Most Christians have a vague notion of the concept that the name of Jesus supposedly has power. But does it? If so, how is that power accessed? Simply by speaking that phrase out loud? How is it that a name has power? Is "in the name of Jesus" simply a formulaic verbal expression which God requires us to use in order to manifest forth the power and authority of Jesus Christ? That just seems so, so superficial! But what is the spiritual reality behind the idea of there being accessible power in the name of Jesus? Let's take a look.

> *Who* (Jesus), *being in the form of God* (spirit), *thought being equal with God not something to be grasped at as plunder; But made himself of no reputation, and took upon him the form of a servant and was made in the likeness of men; And being found in fashion as a man* (this expression simply means he was a man), *he humbled himself, and became obedient unto death, even the death of the cross. Wherefore God also has highly exalted him, and given him the name which is above every name; That at the name of Jesus every knee should bow, of things in heaven, and in earth, and under the earth; And that every tongue should confess that Jesus Christ is Lord, to the glory of God the Father. (Philippians 2:6-10)*

Why and when did God give Jesus "the name which is above every name?" It was because of and after he'd lived his whole life with the yoke of humility and meekness to his heavenly Father unto the death of the cross. In contrast, Jesus got his name "Jesus" because of the angel's command (Matthew 1:21) at the time of his birth (Matthew 1:25). So this "name which is above every name" can not be the actual name "Jesus."

You may think, "But it then says, "That at the name of Jesus every knee should bow, ..." and you'd be right. Let's stop and take a closer look at "the name of Jesus." The little word "of" holds the key to proper understanding here. This word "of" usually represents (as it does here) the genitive case, of which there are 8 or more different kinds. "The cup of coffee" is the genitive of contents. "The cup of my wife" is the genitive of possession. "The cup of porcelain" is the genitive of material.

Most believe (including me for a long time) that this "at the name of Jesus" is the genitive of apposition ... that is, "at the name which is Jesus." But by the context this must be the genitive of possession, because it just said that God gave the name to Jesus, which would mean that now Jesus owns or possesses it. This phrase should be understood as "the name which belongs to Jesus." And what is this name?

We have an expression, "Stop in the name of the law." We know that doesn't mean that the actual word "law" has any authority or power, but rather "the name of the law" means all the power and authority the law represents. The name which belongs to Jesus represents all the power and authority given to him by God after his death, resurrection and ascension! This name was bestowed upon Jesus upon his being seated at the right hand of God. If any "name" sums up all this authority, it would be "Lord."

This Jesus has God raised up, of which we all are witnesses.

Therefore being by the right hand of God (which represents his active authority over His creation) *exalted, and having received of the Father the promise of* ("which is" - genitive of apposition) *the holy spirit, He has shed forth this, which you now see and hear. Therefore let all the house of Israel know assuredly, that God has made that same Jesus, whom you have crucified, both Lord and Christ. (Acts 2:32, 33, 36)*

Jesus was made Christ (the Anointed One) on the very day of Luke 4:18ff. He was made Lord after his death and resurrection, upon being seated at the right hand of God, which occurred during the ten days between his ascension and the day of Pentecost.

This same word, "exalted" is used both here in Acts and back in Philippians 2, tying both sections together. Now we're going to take a look at two short sections from the gospel of John which will not only tie together this receiving and sending of the holy spirit by Jesus, but also help us understand the power and authority of the name which is above every name which Jesus was given.

But the Comforter, which is the holy spirit, which the Father will send in my name, he shall teach you all things, and bring all things to your remembrance, whatsoever I have said unto you. (John 14:26)

But when the Comforter is come, whom I will send unto you from (para - from beside) the Father, even the spirit of truth, which proceeds from (para - from beside) the Father, he shall testify of me. (John 15:26)

Jesus sending the spirit from beside (*para*) the Father is the exact same as the Father sending the spirit in (*en*) Jesus' name. The Father would send us the promise of the spirit in (*en* - the vehicle being) the power and authority over heaven and earth which would be given to His son, Jesus; that is, in Jesus' lordship. This is also stated by Jesus saying he would send the Comforter from beside his Father; that is, while seated at his Father's right hand. This seating at the right hand of God was Jesus' glorification, and did not happen until after he died in his perfection, rose, and ascended into heaven.

> *But this he spoke of the spirit, which they who believe on him should receive; for the holy spirit was not yet given, because that Jesus was not yet glorified. (John 7:39)*

Confessing, or acknowledging the lordship (power and authority) of Jesus, places you under his authority, thus opening you completely up to becoming a recipient of everything good which God has intended for you but can only supply to you in and by means of the lordship (name) of Jesus.

> *That if you shall confess with your mouth the Lord Jesus, believing in your heart that God has raised him from the dead, you shall be saved* (made whole)*; For with the heart man believes unto righteousness, and with the mouth, confession is made unto salvation. (Romans 10:9, 10)*

This is what it means that God sends us the spirit in the name of Jesus, that Jesus sends us the spirit from (beside) his Father. The spiritual authority (lordship) of Jesus is the means by which all good things are given to us by God, for God has fully vested all good things in His son, and given him the authority to share those good things with whoever will receive it.

> *And whatsoever you do in word or deed, do all in the name of the Lord Jesus, giving thanks to God and the Father by means of him. (Colossians 3:17)*

Now you know this doesn't mean, as I walk down the street, "I now move my foot in the name of the Lord Jesus. I now breathe in the name of the Lord Jesus. Etc. Etc." It means I walk in the spiritual authority which belongs to Jesus and is the means by which all good things are and have been given to me by God. I have to take this right upon myself and exercise it. I have confessed Jesus as my Lord, as my authority; therefore, I am subject to and am a recipient of his wisdom, revelation and power. I have a right to it, a right to claim it, a right to express it and walk in the reality of its power and authority.

> *Who* (God) *has delivered us from the authority of darkness, and has transferred us into the kingdom of the Son of His love. (Colossians 1:13)*

Only by partaking of a continual spiritual growth of (genitive of contents) the revelation of the Christ within, can we hope to effectively partake of the benefits of the supreme authority bestowed upon Jesus after his resurrection.

> *That the God of our Lord Jesus Christ, the Father of glory; may give unto you the spirit of wisdom and revelation in the intimate experiential knowing (epignosko) of him; The eyes of your heart being enlightened; that you may know what is … the exceeding greatness of his power toward us to believe, according to the working of His mighty power, Which he wrought in Christ, when he raised him from the dead, and set him at His own right hand in the heavenlies* (the spiritual realm), *Far above all principality and authority, and might, and dominion, and every name that is named, not only in this world, but also in that which is to come, And has put all things under his feet, and gave him to be the head over all things for the church, Which is his body, the fullness of him who fills all in all. (Ephesians 1:17, 18a, 19-23)*

"In the name of Jesus" simply means our existence in and expression of the power and authority given to the Son of God (after he became obedient unto the death of the cross and by means of his resurrection and subsequent glorification, and which is passed on to us from God by means of the Christ within when and as we partake of his lordship), by means of our humble (and meek) acceptance of his spiritual authority over us. Do all things in the name of the Lord Jesus, giving thanks onto God, our Father, by means of him!

WHY JESUS WAS 40 DAYS IN THE WILDERNESS

Was it wasted time? Definitely not!

Have you ever wondered why Jesus went into the wilderness for 40 days? Here he is, the son of God, sent to save the world, having only a short time in which to fulfill his earthly ministry. Yet God saw fit that His son should spend 40 days and 40 nights away from civilization, away from any opportunity to help or bless people. Why?

Before we can understand why Jesus went into the wilderness, it is necessary to understand the event which immediately preceded it, and its significance. The event which immediately preceded Jesus' journey in the wilderness was that Jesus was baptized by John the Baptist, at which time heaven opened unto him.

> *And it came to pass in those days, that Jesus came from Nazareth of Galilee, and was baptized of John in Jordan. And immediately coming up out of the water, he saw the heavens opened, and the spirit like a dove descending upon him. And there came a voice from heaven, saying, You are my beloved Son, in whom I am well pleased. (Mark 1:9-11)*

The heavens being opened unto Jesus means that he saw spiritually for the first time. Until that time, though he was born of the spirit of God, his only approach to his Father was via the (Old Testament) Scriptures. In this he was just like any other man who lived at that time.

His baptism by John fully represented what happens to us when we are baptized by the Spirit. He went into the water a physical being, limited by his mind and understanding, but he came out "reborn" as a spiritual being, with the heavens (the spiritual realm) opened to him, with direct access to his Father, God.

> *And Jesus, when he was baptized, went up immediately out of the water; and, lo, the heavens were opened unto him, and he saw the spirit of God descending like a dove, and lighting upon him; and lo a voice from heaven, saying, This is my beloved Son, in whom I am well pleased. (Matthew 3:16, 17)*

So far, only Jesus has seen the Spirit of God descending like a dove (it doesn't say the spirit looked like a dove, but rather descended like a dove) upon him. But in John we learn that John the Baptist also saw what Jesus saw, and we learn why.

> *And John bare record, saying, I saw the spirit descending from heaven like a dove, and it abode upon him. And I knew him not (as being the Messiah); but He that sent me to baptize with water, the same said unto me, Upon whom you shall see the spirit descending, and remaining on him, the same is he who baptizes with the holy spirit. And I saw, and bare record that this is the son of God. (John 1:32-34)*

John did not look at Jesus and know that he was the son of God. Seeing by the spirit the holy spirit of God descending upon Jesus, that was the proof, the spiritual experience, the knowing in his heart that Jesus was the son of God, because God had told him that would be the proof.

The first thing God ever told His son directly was that he was His beloved son, and that He was well pleased in him (another way of translating this is "This is my son, the beloved, in whom I have found delight."). The first things God confirmed to Jesus, upon achieving the ability to directly communicate with him, was that 1) he was His son; 2) he was beloved by Him, and 3) in him (that is, inside him) He was delighted.

Now we can address the reason Jesus went into the wilderness.

> *Then was Jesus led up of the Spirit into the wilderness to be tempted* (being tempted) *of the devil. And when he had fasted forty days and forty nights, he was afterward hungry. (Matthew 4:1)*

> *And immediately the spirit drives him* (to cast out, with the idea of force) *into the wilderness. And he was there in the wilderness forty days, tempted of Satan; and was with the wild beasts; and the angels ministered unto him. (Mark 1:12, 13)*

> *And Jesus being full of the holy spirit returned from Jordan, and was led by the spirit into the wilderness. Being forty days tempted of the devil. And in those days he did eat nothing; and when they were ended, he afterward hungered. (Luke 4:1, 2)*

This was not Jesus' idea to go into the wilderness, it was his Father's. It was the spirit of God which "led" him or even "drives" him into the wilderness.

In all of these records is indicated that the spirit of God was with Jesus every moment of every one of those forty days and nights. At no time did his Father ever desert him or leave him alone. God was always with His son, and Jesus always walked, from the time of his baptism by John, in the spiritual awareness of his Father's love and delight in him.

In Mark we see an immediacy and an intensity not seen in the other two records. This was something that God wanted to happen in his son's life right away. What was that? To be alone with Him, and to be tempted by the devil. The second thing Jesus needed to experience (after learning of his Father's love for and delight in him) was how his enemy works. Jesus needed to learn to recognize the voice and the methods of his (and his Father's) enemy.

Why forty days? The number forty (40) is seen a number of times in the Bible as a period of trial, of a testing in order to be cleansed or refined and perfected; like products are tested and their flaws corrected in order to ensure their capability and durability. In Noah's time it rained 40 days and 40 nights. In Moses' time, after thinking he could save Israel his way, Moses fled to and lived in Midian for 40 years, returning to deliver Israel God's way. Also, after rejecting the idea that the Promised Land was theirs for the taking, Israel wandered in the wilderness 40 years, until all those who did not believe died, after which Israel entered into the Promised Land. After Jesus was raised from the dead he remained on the earth for 40 days before he ascended off it.

In the case of Jesus, the ability to access heaven and his Father directly also meant the ability to recognize and deal with the devil and all the devil's spirits directly. Before beginning his earthly ministry, Jesus had to be tested by his spiritual enemy. It was in the wilderness, away from people, that Jesus not only powerfully drew close to his Father, but also stood against the devil and defeated him, so that this seasoned ability would be completely at his disposal as he fulfilled his responsibilities as the Christ.

> *For this purpose the son of God was manifested* (which began at his baptism by John when he was manifested to John as being the son of God), *that he might destroy the works of the devil* (the doing of which began in the wilderness immediately afterward). *(I John 3:8b)*

Since Adam, no other man besides Jesus ever addressed the devil directly. That's because no other man had heaven completely opened unto him. (If you have any questions concerning how the devil and his spirits dwell in heaven, please go to the website www. givemechrist.com and read the study Where is Heaven and When do we get there?)

The ministry of Jesus as the Christ could not begin until Jesus, as God's manifested spiritual son had been successfully tested by (and thus had learned to clearly recognize and defeat) Satan (the devil and all his spiritual host of devil spirits).

Only after his successful stand against the devil in the wilderness, Jesus having manifestly acquired and operated power over the evil one, was he anointed to be and began his earthly ministry as the Christ.

> *And Jesus returned* (from the wilderness) *in the power of the spirit into Galilee ... And he came to Nazareth ... And there was delivered unto him the scroll of the prophet Isaiah. And when he had opened the scroll, he found the place where it was written, The Spirit of the Lord is upon me, because he has anointed me* (verb form of "Christ") *to preach the gospel to the poor; he has sent me to heal the brokenhearted, to preach deliverance to the captives, and recovering of sight to the blind, to set at liberty them that are bruised, To preach the acceptable year of the Lord. And he began to say unto them, This day is this scripture fulfilled in your ears. (Luke 4:14a, 16a, 17-19, 21)*

In too many church bodies today, those that seem to represent the things of God, by teaching and preaching and exerting authority over others, have not been successfully tested by the devil. Though they have been taught the Bible and how to teach it and how to administer the things of their denomination, heaven has not been opened unto them so that they are able to learn to recognize the voice of their enemy and to stand against him. And so the devil's ways get mixed with God's ways.

> *A bishop* (overseer) *then must be blameless, ... Not a novice, lest being lifted up with pride he fall into devilish judgments* (decisions). *(I Timothy 3:2a, 6)*

Every man and woman who desires to serve the living God by the spirit must of necessity, at some point in their spiritual education and according to God's timetable, go through a period of testing by the devilish principalities and powers of the heavenly realm and come away cleansed and strengthened by God on the other side. When they do, the service to the body which Christ works in their heart and life can be carried out successfully and powerfully, freer from the deceit of the enemy of God.

IS JESUS THE ONLY WAY TO GOD

Yes, No and Yes

The short answer to the question posed by this study's title is: Yes and No. Yes Jesus is the only way to know God as Father, which comes when the life of God's son becomes your own life, thereby making you also God's son and God also your father. God can be known without Jesus Christ, but only as a lord and taskmaster, as He was in the Old Testament. A true understanding of Him without the spirit of Jesus Christ is impossible, but rather will be cloudy at best. Understanding His methods and intentions truly will be impossible and often seem contradictory. Whether you know God as father or lord, either way, Jesus Christ is the only way to live forever; either by receiving his life today in this age by believing unto him; or at one of the two resurrections, when man will be judged by God (via Jesus) according to his works, and either given eternal life at that time, or be consigned eternal death.

> *Jesus says unto him* (Thomas) *I am the way, the truth, and the life; no man comes unto* (pros - toward) *the Father, but by me.* *(John 14:6)*

This is the verse which many use for their belief that the only way to God is by believing in Jesus Christ. But this verse does not say "God," it says "the Father." There were many people in the Old Testament, all of whom lived before Jesus Christ, who had a fairly good (at least at times) relationship with God; not as Father but rather as Lord. They didn't come to God by Jesus. Are they all to be damned?

For preaching about this cult leader (Jesus) to the crowds, Peter and John were thrown into jail overnight and then brought before some of the same politically powerful men who had the Romans kill Jesus, and were questioned as to what right they had to preach Jesus. Peter finished his spirit-inspired reply by boldly proclaiming,

> *Neither is there salvation in any other; for there is none other name under heaven given among men, whereby we must be saved. (Acts 4:12)*

Salvation is only by means of Jesus Christ. Is salvation the same as knowing God? No. Is salvation the same as living forever? Close. One of salvation's most important aspects is victory over death; and whether one believes unto Jesus and receives the spiritual adoption of God and His (eternal) life now, in this age, or receives that life at one of the two resurrections in the future, life after and victory over death is only possible because of and by means of Jesus Christ.

> *Jesus said unto her* (Martha, just before raising her brother Lazarus from the dead), *I am the resurrection, and the life; he who believes unto me, though he were dead, yet shall he live: (John 11:25)*

Many quote John 3:16, and this verse does indicate that everlasting life comes to a person by believing unto Jesus as the Christ, the son of God. This verse however, of itself, does not indicate that Jesus is the only way to God, or to everlasting life.

> *For God so loved the world, that He gave His only begotten son,*

that whosoever believes in (eis - unto) him should not perish, but have everlasting life. (John 3:16)

Jesus himself proclaimed again and again that he had been sent by God to reclaim mankind for God. Following are but a couple of the many examples to be found in the four Gospels.

I am the living bread which came down from heaven; if any man eat of this bread he shall live forever; and the bread that I will give is my flesh, which I will give for the life of the world. (John 6:51)

He who believes on (eis - unto) him (God's son) is not condemned; but he who believes not is condemned already, because he has not believed in (eis - unto) the name of the only begotten son of God. (John 3:18)

So far we have read that no man comes to God as Father but by means of Jesus Christ. We've learned that believing unto Jesus Christ as being God's son is the means of receiving everlasting life; of not perishing but living forever. Now the question is whether or not people who never believed unto Jesus Christ, even in this age, will or can ever receive everlasting life; and can they ever know the true God, though they never believed unto Jesus as being the Christ.

Surprisingly, the answers to the above seem to be yes and yes. Jesus himself had this to say:

For as the Father has life in Himself; so has He given to the son to have life in himself; And has given him authority to execute judgment also, because he is the son of man. Marvel not at this; for the hour is coming, in the which all that are in the graves shall hear his voice. And shall come forth; they who have done good, unto the resurrection of life; and they who have done evil, unto the resurrection of damnation. (John 5:26-29)

Jesus is speaking of the two resurrections (which do not include the gathering together of the saints, also known as the rapture). Notice that he says, "... they who have done good ..." and "... they who have done evil ... ." Here he does not mention anything about the need to believe unto him, only the judging of men's doings. So it seems that those who have done good (enough, according to the judgment of God) will be raised in the resurrection to live forever. This is confirmed in the book of Revelation.

> *And I saw the dead, small and great, stand before God; and the books were opened; and another book was opened, which is the book of life; and the dead were judged out of those things which were written in the books, according to their works. And the sea gave up the dead which were in it; and death and hell delivered up the dead which were in them; and they were judged every man according to their works. And death and hell were cast into the lake of fire. This is the second death. And whosoever was not found written in the book of life was cast into the lake of fire. (Revelation 20:12-15)*

Again, in the resurrection men shall be judged by their works, not simply by whether or not they had faith in Jesus Christ. The following section from the book of Romans reaffirms this very truth.

> *For as many as have sinned without* (outside the) *law shall also perish without law; and as many as have sinned in the law shall be judged by the law; (For not the hearers of the law are just before God, but the doers of the law shall be justified. For when the Gentiles, who have not the law, do by nature the things contained in the law, these having not the law, are a law unto themselves; Who show the work of the law written in their hearts, their conscience also bearing witness, and their thoughts the mean while accusing or else excusing one another;) In the day when God shall judge the secrets of men by Jesus Christ*

according to my gospel. (Romans 2:12-16)

Note that the above section speaks of the judgment of Jews and Gentiles, but says nothing of the judgment of the church of God, the born again believers.

What we come to understand from reading all the above is that the only way to know God as Father is by means of receiving the spirit of His son, Jesus the Christ. To those who have believed unto Jesus Christ as the son of God, the judgment of God has already declared us to be righteous and holy beings, due to our union with *the* righteous and holy being, Christ. To us who have been born of the righteousness of Christ, we will be gathered together with him (whether alive or dead at the time he returns for us) before the resurrections and judgments spoken of in Revelation.

> *Even the righteousness of God which is by faith of Jesus Christ unto all and upon all them who believe; for there is no difference* (between Jew & Gentile)*; For all have sinned, and come short of the glory of God; Being justified freely by His grace through the redemption that is in Christ Jesus; (Romans 3:22-24)*

> *For the Lord* (Jesus) *himself shall descend from heaven with a shout, with the voice of the archangel, and with the trump of God; and the dead in Christ shall rise first; Then we who are alive and remain shall be caught up together with them in the clouds, to meet the Lord in the air; and so shall we ever be with the Lord. (I Thessalonians 4:16, 17)*

To all others, whether they knew God as a lord and taskmaster or not at all, they shall be judged by their works and either be consigned to the second death (where there will be no consciousness) or granted eternal life, handed to them by Jesus Christ at the resurrection and judgment of God. So even if they don't believe unto him in this life, it is still by means of Jesus Christ that they receive eternal life.

Which would you rather have: God as loving, generous Father? Or God as harsh, demanding taskmaster? Raised to ever be with Christ who is your life, having been granted the righteousness of Christ as a free gift when you believed unto him as God's son? Or standing before God and His son Jesus and be judged for your works, the determination of eternal life or death hanging over you?

Can you know God without Jesus Christ? Yes, but not as a loving Father, only a lord and master, like those who lived in the Old Testament. Can the final judgment be avoided? Yes. The final judgment for those who have Christ has already been handed down - justified, righteous! We who have believed unto Jesus as the Christ have already received his eternal life as our own!

> *Set your affection on things above, not on things on the earth. For you are dead, and your life is hid with Christ in God. When Christ, our life, shall appear, then shall you also appear with him in glory. (Colossians 3:2-4)*

The only way to live forever is through the resurrection power of the Lord Jesus Christ. That can become yours now, today, before his return, where you will come to know God as a loving Father. If not today, then the best you can hope for is to know God as a lord, as you live your life in the condemnation of sin and spiritual darkness, waiting for the judgment of your works at one of the two resurrections by Jesus Christ before the throne of God, where either you will receive everlasting life, or you will receive everlasting death.

It is not for me or for any other man to make that judgment of another. (Only one man, the Son of Man, Jesus Christ, has been awarded that right and responsibility). But it *is* for me to make known the choices you have in life. May you believe unto Jesus Christ, not only today but all your days, and learn to enjoy the eternal, righteous life which is freely yours in Christ.

That in the administration of the fullness of times He might gather together in one all things in Christ, both which are in heaven, and which are on earth; even in him. (Ephesians 1:10)

VANITY

The accomplishment of nothing by the energetic
expression of a self-centered heart

VANITY OF THE MIND

Vanity or sanity, you choose

This I say therefore, and testify in the Lord, that you no longer walk as the Gentiles are walking in the vanity of their mind. (Ephesians 4:17)

This exhortation in Ephesians to not live out your life like pagan unbelievers do, seeking only to please themselves and satisfy their ungodly logic, comes immediately on the heels of the description of how to grow spiritually in the body of Christ. Ephesians 4:11-16 spells out the how of growing up to be a spiritual adult. From being tended to by the gift ministries that Jesus Christ himself is supplying to his body, to becoming spiritually mature and equipped to do the same for others, directly connected to the head, Jesus Christ.

This word "vanity" is the Greek word *mataios*, and means without purpose, empty as to results, fruitless. Working out at the gym in order to increase fitness is not vain, is not fruitless. Your body gets stronger, you're able to do more. On the other hand, if your time at the gym is only so that you'll think that others are thinking that you look good, then you are serving the vanity of your mind.

When your thoughts, words and/or deeds are merely an expression of your feelings, without a purposeful intent to accomplish something, this is vanity of the mind. Any and all responses to the influence of the working of Satan fall into this category.

This vain expression goes nowhere, and is an end in and of itself. Worry, fear, lust (vain desire), rage, envy, bitterness; all the thinking which is influenced by these and other strong passions as an end in themselves, are vanity of the mind. They accomplish nothing, and the result is corruption and decay … a getting worse.

Why did you lash out in anger at your child? Merely because anger demanded that you act on itself. Was it useful? No. It was vanity. Why do you get depressed? Because depression comes and demands an important place in your mind and heart, and so you allow it. Vanity! It produces no results, only corruption and decay. Why do you argue politics? Because strife demands that it be acted upon! This is vanity.

We can be choosing thoughts based on where they will take us and what they will produce in our lives. A young woman once told me that she had decided to judge her thoughts based on where they wanted to take her, and she said life immediately became so much easier and more powerful. She also said that she got the strong thought that judging her thoughts in this manner was "cheating" and "not being honest."

See how the devil deceives? He says, "What you're doing (which is working well) is being dishonest." While, "Keep doing what you're doing. Even though it doesn't work and never has, at least you're being honest." So you see how the devil wants to be the judge of your thoughts? Of course he judges the thoughts he has inspired in your heart as being right and honest, and God's thoughts as being dishonest and wrong! He has been this way since Adam & Eve were in the garden, when he deceived them into eating of the fruit of the tree of the knowledge of good and evil.

Vanity of the mind does not discern rightly, rather giving in to the easiest or most powerful thoughts ... based on vain logic ... which is often based on nothing more than the examples we had growing up, and the strong feelings thus produced in us! Since the feelings that come in these situations are strong, we give in to them, allowing them to justify their presence in our lives. Yet they are vanity.

Stress, now there's a big one. Stress occurs because you've decided something is worth stressing about. How full of itself is stress! Why, it struts around thinking it is accomplishing something, when it accomplishes nothing but corruption and decay ... it weakens you, makes you sick, kills you! It even tells you it is being useful, that it is helping you get things done! Why do you give in to it? Do you think you have no choice? In Christ you do!

Try to fly, with no outside resource. Vanity. Lots of effort, no results. You can't do life on your own - successfully, fruitfully - any more than an apple tree can produce fruit without air, water, sunshine, nutrients. You need help. Your life's been designed to require outside resources!

You, and all of creation, have been designed to live life resourced by the presence & power of God. To restore this original design in all of creation is the purpose and accomplishment of God's Christ, Jesus.

Romans 1:18-32 contains the record of the fall of Lucifer, as expressed in and through the lives of mankind, God's greatest creation. Verses 21 & 22 contain wonderful information regarding our study today.

> *Because that, when they knew God, they glorified Him not as God, neither were thankful; but became vain in their imaginations* (logical reasonings), *and their foolish heart was darkened. Professing themselves to be wise, they became fools. (Romans 1:21, 22)*

It seems that the last step on the road down into fruitless thinking is turning the mind away from the recognition of God's providing for you. Thankfulness is a real, visceral response to the receiving of a gift. In fact, the Aramaic word for thankfulness is literally "receipt of a kindness." Turning away from thankfulness is a closing of oneself to God, and in its place comes vanity! Trying to fulfill yourself by your own efforts ... it cannot be done.

This describes exactly what happened when Adam & Eve ate of the tree of the knowledge of good and evil. By eating of this "tree", man fell into "vain imaginations" ("imaginations" is the Greek word logizmos - logical reasonings).

As you continue reading through the rest of this first chapter of Romans, you can see that God spends a lot of time on the uselessness and harm of homosexual sex. It produces nothing! Homosexual sex can not produce offspring, so it is literally a fruitless endeavor, meant only for vain pleasure! God is not against pleasure, but never as an end in itself. The vain pursuit of pleasure as an end in itself is the cause of a mass amount of harm, destruction and decay in this world.

> *For the creation was made subject to vanity (not willingly, but by reason of him who did the subjecting* (Satan, in the garden)*) in hope, Because the creation itself also shall be delivered from the bondage of corruption into the glorious liberty of the children of God. (Romans 8:20, 21)*

Life, and all of creation, was designed by God to require the continuous supply that comes with a connection with God. When man, and all of creation, was subjected to vanity by Satan, everything began to die, because that connection with the supplier of life was broken. In Christ, everything is once again made alive, reconnected with God, brought back into that state of harmonious accord with the ever-flowing supply of God.

(Jesus said) *He that believes on me, as the scripture has said, out of his belly shall flow rivers of living water. (John 7:38)*

(Jesus said) *But whosoever drinks of the water that I shall give him shall never thirst; but the water that I shall give him shall be in him a well of water springing up into everlasting life. (John 4:14)*

God designed life to be lived from out of His Own fullness. Man vainly reasons and lives, seeking to fulfill himself without that connection to God's limitless supply. It would be like taking a plant out of soil and water and air and expecting it to grow and produce fruit. Vanity!

Religions, and even "Churchianity" (the man-organized Christian church) have come into being, and are maintained, primarily by vanity of the mind.

(Jesus is speaking to the Pharisees … the religious sect which interpreted the proper application of the law of Moses) *You hypocrites, well did Isaiah prophesy of you, saying, This people draws near unto me with their mouth, and honors me with their lips; but their heart is far from me. But in vain they do worship me, teaching for doctrines the commandments of men. (Matthew 15:7-9)*

"Going through the motions" is vanity. Going through the motions that you have decided, by your vain reasonings, are what God should want out of you, is vanity! Going to church on Sunday, just so you won't feel bad about yourself, is an example of vanity!

Casting down imaginations (logizmos – logical reasonings) and every high thing that exalts itself contrary to the experiential knowing (gnosis) of God, and bringing into captivity every thought into the obedience which is Christ. (II Corinthians 10:5)

This is our "job" as believers of Christ, as those who trust that what God has supplied us through Jesus Christ is the way life is meant to be lived. Cast down (as an enemy) all vain reasoning, which began at the tree of the knowledge of good and evil with Adam and Eve. Don't seek to reason out what is right and what is wrong by yourself, what is good and what is bad. Don't seek to fulfill yourself by your own efforts. Don't settle for a life of merely expressing vain feelings and passions; rather, seek the experience of God our Father, which is found only in Christ Jesus, our Lord.

CONSTIPATED CONSCIOUSNESS

All stopped up inside

Paralysis, callousness and constipation of the soul are the traits of consciousness and character which result from walking in the vanity of the mind.

> *This I say therefore, and testify in the Lord, that you walk not as* (other) *Gentiles walk, in the vanity of their mind. Having the understanding darkened, being alienated from the life of God through the ignorance that is in them, because of the blindness of their heart: Who being past feeling have given themselves over unto lasciviousness, to work all uncleanness with greediness.* (Ephesians 4:17-19)

There are a number of very descriptive terms in this short section, which visually and accurately describe the developing quality of a person's consciousness and character as they live out their lives with their own thinking exalted to the throne of God.

> *walk* – to go from one place to another; here used of one's thinking.

other – The King James has this word just before the word Gentiles. Most texts omit this word, as I have.

Gentiles – literally, "the nations" .... every human being except those born of Israel or those born of the spirit of God.

vanity – empty as to results, fruitless, without fruitful purpose, useless

mind – nous, the organ of mental perception and thought

understanding – dianoia, from the same root as "mind", means a thinking through, figuring things out

darkened – literally, this phrase reads "being darkened in the ability to figure things out."

alienated – literally, to become "other than."

life – *zoe*, life in general

of God – which is God's, owned by God, which is God's makeup, or nature

through – *dia*, by means of, on account of

ignorance – *agnosis*, lacking any experience with or personal knowledge of

because of – *dia* (same word as "through")

blindness – *porosis*, hardening, callousness

heart – where the Greeks believed the real self resided, the part of the mind that believes

being past feeling – to put off the feeling of pain, be paralyzed

given themselves over unto – surrendered to

lasciviousness – licentiousness, no boundaries or limits

uncleanness – *akatharsis* – that which stops up, prevents flow or expulsion – constipation

greediness – insatiable craving

Following is a translation of Ephesians 4:17-19 using the definitions above:

"Everyone in the world who is not walking by either an external moral code which deals with the flesh (Israel) or by the spirit of God (the church of God) are instead going from one place to another in their mind in the fruitlessness of their own thinking which is continually endeavoring to control, order, understand and save the world (trying to be God) through its own efforts. The result of this fruitless quest is a mental feeling around in the dark with no experience of the life of God (which is the true light of mankind), which they cannot experience because the seat of their personal life has become calloused. Being thus paralyzed from any feeling, they have surrendered themselves completely to an ever increasingly empty, unfulfilling life with no boundaries, resulting in a constipation of thought and character which continues to grow worse and worse as they pursue their vanities with an insatiable craving."

Trapped in a life where that stopped up feeling, that constipation of consciousness never goes away, where I have to try harder and harder in order to feel anything, where my actions are more and more outrageous, but where I feel less and less any satisfaction, I cannot seem to figure out any why's or wherefore's, but rather am caught in a deadening cycle of endeavoring and failing, where nothing is clearly seen and no way out shows itself. I am like a dead body trapped in a coffin, and the life and light of God are but words with no meaning.

But you have not so learned Christ. If so be that you have heard him and have been taught by him, as the truth is in Jesus. (Ephesians 4:20, 21)

I'll let you read how the new man can take the place of the old man, which is laid out in the verses following. These verses paint quite a different picture than what came immediately before!

Life was never meant to be lived in vanity, with our own thinking and feeling at the center of all that is true. Unlike the lying promise of Satan in the garden, we are not God and we will never be God. Trying to be Him and do what only He can do is what makes our lives miserable and eventually kills us.

In our physical lives we eat and drink and pee and poop; we breathe in and out. There is a flow, in and out. And so with the life of God. We receive, we give, we share, we let go of all things not beneficial, or when the benefit has ended; we share what is beneficial, knowing that the One who gave it originally will continue to give more. This is a life which is quite opposite that of the nations, but it *is* the life designed by God and made available to us by Jesus Christ.

We don't need to hoard physical possessions or feelings of contentment and security, or even bad feelings. We know God will give us what we need for our benefit, when and as we need it, and enough to share with others. The spirit of Christ is the (super)natural laxative for our life; our thinking, our feeling, our understanding and our human experience. Seek Christ continually and your life will flow with the life, the light and the love of God.

THE ILLUSION OF CONTROL
A real trick of the mind

The quality of our life is determined by where we direct our efforts.

How much time and effort do you spend figuring out ways to get someone to do what you want them to do? Or to get them to stop doing what you don't want them to do? (all for their own benefit, of course!). Or to have a situation happen exactly as you want it to happen? And what are the results? Stress, conflict, tension, guilt, poor relationships, frustration, anger ... and worse! And why do you do it? In order to satisfy some need to be in control of the world around you. Because the world is constantly telling you that you need to become a master at being in control of your surroundings in order to live a full rich meaningful life. What a lie!

Only Christ can give you the peace and harmony you so desire. Come to the place in your life where your peace and satisfaction come from within, in your relationship with God in the spirit of Christ; where your satisfaction is continually flowing out of the love and joy being provided by the presence of Christ.

Let me be clear. If someone else, or something else, has to act a certain way, or be a certain way, in order for you to be at peace in your life, in order for joy to surround and fill you, then you are the one who is out of control.

> *And he* (Jesus) *said unto them* (his disciples), *Take heed, and beware of covetousness; for a man's life consists not in the abundance of things which he possesses. (Luke 12:15)*

When your focus is on a need to control circumstances and/or people in order to have a good life, you will end up wrestling with shadows. Lots of effort, little or no fruitful results. Vanity.

TV shows abound with this fruitless effort, because it causes so much drama. If you know someone who has a lot of this "drama" in their life, it's because they're so wrapped up in trying to control what they cannot, and ignoring the effort to control what they can.

Nowhere in the Bible are we commanded to control another. Reprove, yes. Instruct, yes. Discipline, yes. But control, no. Why do you think God never commands us to try to control another? I mean, has God ever controlled you? No! And yet we can spend so much time and effort trying to do what God Himself will not do!

(The simple reason why we endeavor to do what God Himself will not do is that we have partaken of the fruit of the tree of the knowledge of good and evil, where we act as God, after deciding how God ought to act! In reality, we just want ourselves to feel good.)

> *Not that I speak in respect of want; for I have learned in whatsoever state I am, therewith to be content. I know both how to be abased, and I know how to abound; everywhere and in all things I am instructed both* (how) *to be full and to be hungry, both to abound and to suffer need. I can do all things through Christ who strengthens me. (Philippians 4:11-13)*

The instruction Paul speaks of is spiritual instruction ... from God by means of the spirit of Christ within. God does not teach us how to control our circumstances or the people around us, He teaches us how to be at peace in the spirit of Christ, no matter what the circumstances!

The "mind of the flesh" (fleshly mind, carnal mind) believes that the flesh can provide spiritual results, and so it tries to control that flesh. Rather, on the contrary, the man who seeks to control anyone outside of himself is a man who is at war with God.

> *Because the carnal mind is enmity unto (eis) God; for it is not subject to the law of God, neither indeed can be. So then they are in the flesh cannot please God. (Romans 8:7, 8)*

Here's an example you may be familiar with and which I have all too often run across. Sincere Christians, even pastors of organized churches, seek to control people close to them (children, mate, subordinates, etc.), because "what would it look like?" or "What would other people think?" If you're going to live at peace with God, at peace within yourself, you're going to have to become more concerned with pleasing God than with pleasing others.

> *For do I now persuade men, or God? Or do I seek to please men? For if I yet* (made the effort to) *pleased men, I would not be the servant of Christ. (Galatians 1:10)*

The control we truly seek is only found in being at peace with God, where no thing and no one can knock us off balance.

> *And be not conformed to this world, but be transformed by the renewing of your mind, that you may prove what is that good and acceptable and perfect will of God. (Romans 12:2)*

Whereas there is nothing in this world that can give us the peace and fullness we truly seek, those very things are automatically ours as a part of the gift of Christ within.

> *For he (Christ) is our peace ... (Ephesians 2:14a)*

That Christ may dwell in your hearts by faith; that you being rooted and grounded in love, May be able to comprehend with all saints what is the breadth and length and depth and height; And to know the love of Christ, which passes knowledge (better translated "which is the ultimate human experience"), *that you might be filled with all the fullness of God. (Ephesians 3:17-19)*

What is it you really want in life? Do you really want everyone close to you to live the life you think they ought to live, to do the things you think they ought to do? All so that you'll feel better about your own life? Really? Or what is more likely is that you simply want them to be content and fulfilled in their own life. With that in mind, do you really think you can give that contentment to them by seeking to control their behavior? Can you *make* them have it? Can you live their life for them? If not, then what really are your options?

Be anxious for nothing; but in everything by prayer and supplication (specific requests) *with thanksgiving let your requests be made known unto God. And the peace of God, which passes all* (fleshly) *understanding, shall guard your hearts and minds* (thinking) *through Christ Jesus. (Philippians 4:6, 7)*

You be in control of your thoughts and feelings (yes, feelings). Learn that control, practice trusting your spiritual Father to take care of that which you cannot, to carry the load that you cannot; to work in the hearts and lives (like you can not) of those you love, and to give you the wisdom to see your inability to control. This is where your real strength and control lies.

Therefore I take pleasure in infirmities, in reproaches, in necessities, in persecutions, in distresses for Christ's sake; for when I am weak, then am I strong. (II Corinthians 12:19)

In conclusion, please read this following section from Colossians as being applied to the subject of this study: That you cannot control any other, only the choices you make, the thoughts you think, the feelings you carry around. And understand that the consequences of trying to control what you cannot control will result in many hurtful, destructive feelings and passions and relationships.

> *But now you also put off all these; anger, wrath, malice blasphemy, filthy communication out of your mouth. Lie not one to another, seeing that you have put off the old man with his doings* (which all try to control others and the world around for personal gain)*; And have put on the new man, which is renewed in knowledge* (epignosis - intimate relational knowing)*, according to* (the supply of which is) *the image of him* (God) *who created him* (the new man – Christ in you)*; .... Put on therefore as the elect of God holy and beloved bowels* (out of which the strong feelings and emotions were thought to flow) *of mercies, kindness, humbleness of mind, meekness, longsuffering; Forbearing one another and forgiving one another; if any man have a quarrel against any; even as Christ forgave you, so also do you; And above all these things put on love, which is the bond of perfectness. And let the peace of God rule* (be the arbiter, the decider) *in your hearts, to the which also you are called in one body; and be thankful. (Colossians 3:8-10, 12-15)*

You have been designed to have control of your choices, which determine your part in your relationship with God. Any other control you think you have is but an illusion.

KICKING THE CORPSE

The new man views the old man with compassionate understanding, not harsh judgmentalism and the desire to punish.

I'm very concerned with the health of the mind and the body which I've been given. Before Christ I was concerned with feeling good, and that's about it. Now, with the mind of Christ which has been supplied to me, and which continues to grow and develop as I nourish it, I have a broader view, a more long term view of my mind and my body. I am thankful for them, while not allowing them to determine my destiny.

I don't spend any time "kicking the corpse." I do not hate that part of me that used to sit on the throne of my life as god, which did not acknowledge and need God, but rather was "without God and without hope." I have been given and am growing into something better, but hating myself (my old self) is not a part of that something better.

> *Lie not one to another, seeing that you have put off the old man with his deeds; (Colossians 3:9)*

To "put off" means to lay aside, as an article of clothing you no longer desire to wear. There is no punishment involved, no self-hatred. Simply lay aside that old man which needs to be right, seeks to stand approved before others, and needs to be in charge and in control of everything.

> *Wherefore seeing we also are compassed about with so great a cloud of witnesses, let us lay aside every weight, and the sin which does so easily beset us, and let us run with patience the race that is set before us; Looking unto Jesus the beginner and finisher of our faith ... (Hebrews 12:1, 2a)*

We lay it aside (same Greek word as in Colossians 3:9). We don't fight with it, disparage it, focus on it or emphasize it in any way. We simply lay it aside as being impractical, vain and unprofitable. That becomes easier and easier to do as we walk in what *is* practical, profitable and makes our lives fruitful.

Why is it that Christians think it is a Godly thing to punish themselves, whether mentally and/or physically? Where did the thought, "I'm just a sinner, saved by grace" come from? Why is it so difficult to receive compliments or accolades; why so abhorrent to take any credit for work well done? It is because of vanity of the mind, which denies God and His gift to us and which rather needs to do sacrifice in order to placate God.

> *And Samuel said* (to Saul), *Has the Lord as great delight in burnt offerings and sacrifices, as in obeying the voice of the Lord? Behold, to obey is better than sacrifice, and to hearken than the fat of rams. For rebellion is as the sin of witchcraft, and stubbornness is as iniquity and idolatry. (I Samuel 15:22, 23a)*

When confronted by sin, the correct response is to turn (back) to Christ, not to punish yourself for your error. (Learn, yes ... punish, no) It is the old, sinful man who is "dead in trespasses and sins" which needs to do sacrifice for its failings. In contrast, the new man lives in the "*fait accompli*" (accomplished work) of the sacrifice of Christ. This is "the obedience of faith" of Romans 16:26 and "the obedience of Christ" of II Corinthians 10:5.

For we preach not ourselves, but Christ Jesus the Lord; and ourselves your servants for Jesus' sake. (II Corinthians 4:5)

Most Christians would relate to the first half of this verse, but ignore the second. The worth we have as individuals certainly does not lie in our mere physical and mental existence, for all people, by definition, have those. Rather, our worth as individuals lies in our relationship to God, which exists only in Christ Jesus our Lord. To deny that very real spiritual worth is to deny the gift which God gave us and for which Christ paid the price.

Who do you think you are? That phrase, cast as a challenge, usually leaves the one it has been directed toward at a loss for words. But I now ask you, Who *do* you think you are? Are you a saint or a sinner? Are you a sinner saved by grace, or are you a saint who occasionally sins, who may even now be trapped in a sin? How you honestly answer this question will tell you a lot about what is most important in your life. If you are a sinner saved by grace, then you define yourself by your fleshly thinking and behavior. If you are a saint, then in the self-realization that a new creation has been birthed and is developing within you, you are reaching forth into heaven, seeking to daily lay hold of the spiritual inheritance which has been given you as a member of God's intimate family, a citizen of the kingdom of God.

Just who are you? This question is always, always answered by who and how you relate to and identify with others. If your identify lies in your relating to your fleshly family and the world in general, then you are very much what you do and how you think. If your identity lies in your relating to the working of the spirit of Christ which take place within you, then you are indeed a son of God and joint-heir with Christ. The transition from the carnal to the spiritual identity is not one which happens overnight. Be patient and be faithful.

> *For if you live after* (are supplied by) *the flesh, you shall die;
> but if you through the spirit do mortify* (treat as dead) *the deeds
> of the body, you shall live. For as many as are led by the spirit
> of God, they are the sons of God. For you have not received*
> (taken unto yourself) *the spirit of bondage to fear even more;
> but you have received the spirit of adoption, by which we cry,
> Oh dear Father my Father! The spirit itself bears witness with
> our spirit that we are the children of God; And if children, then
> heirs; heirs of God, and joint-heirs with Christ; if so be that we
> endure with him, that we may be also glorified together with
> him. (Romans 8:13-17)*

What leads you? What motivates you? This has everything to do with who you think you are. The spirit which was offered to you, which you reached out and took unto yourself by deciding to believe unto Jesus Christ, was not given in order to keep you in a bondage of fear of never being good enough, of being afraid to be or do wrong; rather the role of Christ's spirit in your life is to cause you to reach out in heart-filling joyful anticipation to get more and more of what your most intimate relation ... God Himself ... has promised you and provided for you by means of Christ.

You will not reach out to lay hold of your heavenly inheritance if in your heart you are a sinner saved by grace, but only if you are God's righteous son.

> *Wherefore remember that you being in time past Gentiles in
> the flesh, who are called Uncircumcision by that which is called
> the Circumcision in the flesh made by hands; That at that time
> you were without Christ, being aliens from the commonwealth
> of Israel, and strangers from the covenants of promise, having
> no hope, and without God in the world.(Ephesians 2:11-12)*

It's one thing to remember where you came from, it's another to obstinately demand of yourself that you remain in that same old place.

This is not the will of God, that having been delivered from spiritual corruption and death, you present yourself over and over again to God as still being corrupted and dead. If God has given you life, then you are alive! If God has given you citizenship in heaven, then you are a heavenly being! If God desires you to approach Him in the most intimate of ways as a beloved son, then do so! Anything less is not the will of God, but rather comes out of a heart which has not believed unto Christ Jesus our Lord.

Oh, we will always have a lot to learn, but doesn't every child? Think of your own children ... as much as you love them and hold them close to yourself in the most tender part of your heart, don't they have a lot to learn? Don't they make mistakes, fall short of the mark, live less than you desire? But are they thus any less your beloved child?

> *Brethren I count not myself to have arrived* (in understanding and practice – I know I'm on a journey)*; but this one thing I do, forgetting those things which are behind, and reaching forth unto those things which are before, I press toward the mark for the prize of the high calling of God in Christ Jesus. Let us therefore, as many as be perfect* (spiritually grown up)*, be thus minded. (Philippians 3:13-15a)*

This is who we are. This is what we do. Accept the gift of God which is in Christ Jesus our Lord. We are sons of God and joint heirs with Christ. We learn from our every experience, with God as our Father and His spirit as our teacher. We reach forth to acquire more and more of what God has called us to be and have and be able to do. We often fall short, we head off in the wrong direction, but we never quit, for we are sons of God, called to have everything Christ is and has and can do.

Berating your old self is not the will of God. Focusing on and nourishing the new self is.

GRACE

Intentional generosity

GRACE, GIFTS AND THANKFULNESS

All have the same Greek root

Grace, gift and thankfulness are all related words in the Greek.

Grace (*charis* - intentional generosity),

Gift (*charisma* - an expression of *charis*),

Thankfulness (*eucharisma* – the heart's response to the receipt of a *charisma*).

The western man often finds it very difficult to receive a gift thankfully, because he doesn't want to "owe" anyone anything; because the idea of being a "self-made man" is strongly ingrained in his culture. There is also a prevailing attitude of "I'm owed" or "I worked for it" or "I have a right to it."

These are some of the attitudes that make it so difficult to receive gifts. These are some of the attitudes that make it so difficult to receive anything from God. These are some of the attitudes which deprive us of a life of thankfulness.

Perhaps a person doesn't think he deserves the gift. "Aww, you don't have to do that," or "Are you sure?" is often heard from the intended recipient of an offered gift.

> *I* (Paul) *have showed you all things, how that so laboring, you ought to support the weak, and to remember the words of the Lord Jesus, how he said, It is more blessed to give than to receive. (Acts 20:35)*

The giver of the gift gets blessed to give. The receiver of the gift can thus facilitate that blessing in the life of the giver, by being a good receiver of an expression of generosity.

If you want to allow others to get "more blessed," then someone has got to do the receiving! Thankfulness is a visceral response (it affects you) to the receipt of something which is freely given. There is no "you shouldn't have done that" or "are you sure?" in properly receiving a gift which is freely given. There is a heartfelt "Wow, thank you so much for your kind generosity!" Thankfulness is not just receiving the gift being given; it is receiving into the heart the generosity of the giver.

God's ultimate intent in gifting to us from out of His generosity (grace) is that we take on the nature of that generosity.

> *Blessed be the God and Father (the Giver) of our Lord Jesus Christ (the Gift), who has blessed us with all spiritual blessings in the heavenlies in Christ; Unto the praise of His grace's* (generosity's) *glory, wherein He has made us generous* (by means of our response of thankfulness) *in the Beloved. (Ephesians 1:3, 6)*

We actually have a part in blessing God, by being thankful recipients of His gift of Christ. We help facilitate the blessing to God which comes about by allowing Him to give to us! It will take some practice, but one of our primary "jobs" as believers and children of God is to learn to be good receivers of God's generosity.

We are to become excellent recipients of the gifts which flow out of God's grace!

That is what blesses the giver of the gift. And thankfulness completes the cycle of grace, not only giving the receiver of the gift the means to himself give, but also opening his heart to receive more.

> *And as you go, preach, saying, The kingdom of heaven is at hand. Heal the sick, cleanse the lepers, raise the dead, cast out devils; freely you have received, freely give. (Matthew 10:7, 8)*

When Adam and Eve fell, they "fell from grace" because they stopped being thankful for what they had received from God, instead reaching out for what they did not have, believing Satan's lie that what they did not have was important and necessary for them to live a better life. And what was that something better that Satan told them they lacked? Actually, it was vanity of the mind.

> *Because that, when they knew* (by experience) *God, they glorified Him not as God, neither were thankful; but became vain in their logical reasonings, and their foolish heart was darkened. Professing themselves to be wise, they became fools, (Romans 2:21, 22)*

Today is called "the age of grace" by the Apostle Paul. (Ephesians 3:2) Today, God wants to pour out everything He can, everything He is, into your heart and life. And today He is able to do this very thing because of the work of His Son, Jesus Christ. Now it remains for us to become thankful receivers of God's generous gifts! Practice thankfulness and open the door to more of God's grace in your life. A thankful person is rich indeed, for he recognizes the truth that everything he has of value, he has received as a gift.

> *In everything* (of the spirit) *give thanks, for this is the will of God in Christ Jesus concerning you. Quench not the spirit* (by

stopping being thankful). *(I Thessalonians 5:18, 19)*

The best givers of gifts are the best receivers of gifts, and Jesus Christ is our perfect example. Everything he had of value he credited as having been given to him by his Father, God. And in return, he was able to give the ultimate gift for the salvation of the world – his life. He gave it, and today he continues to give it freely to whoever believes on his name.

> *All things that the Father has are mine; therefore said I that he* (the spirit from his Father which he would send) *shall take of mine, and shall show it unto you* (by revelation). *(John 16:15)*

Thank God, Who is the Initiator of all giving, for the gift of His Son Jesus Christ. Thank Jesus Christ for sharing with us all that he has received from his Father. Practice becoming better and better recipients of all the good things of Christ which God, by His spirit, desires to impart unto you. Dwell in the rich rewards of a life of thankfulness, being enriched by God's generosity to the end of sharing your rich spiritual bounty with others. There is no greater life.

FREEDOM FROM SIN'S DOMINATION

Sin is one thing. The domination of sin is another. To be dominated is to be ruled over.

> *Don't you know that to whom you yield yourselves servants to obey, his servants you are to whom you obey; whether of sin unto death, or of obedience unto righteousness? (Romans 6:16)*

Neither sin nor obedience can drag us, kicking and screaming, into its lair. We must yield to it. This is not meant to marginalize the powerful effect of sin, which produces powerful emotions, powerful passions in people.

> *For when we were in the flesh, the motions (pathos - powerful emotions, or passions) of (caused by) sin, which were by the law, did work in our members to bring forth fruit unto death. (Romans 7:5)*

As weird as this sounds, God is saying that the powerful emotions of sin are in people's lives by means of the law ... which He Himself gave to Moses! Whoa! Think about this a little! Check out the next few verses.

> *But now we are delivered from the law, being dead to that* (the law) *wherein we were held; that we should serve in newness of spirit, and not in the oldness of the letter. What shall we say then? Is the law sin? God forbid. No, I wouldn't have known sin, but by the law; for I hadn't known lust, except the law had said, You shall not covet. But sin, taking occasion by the commandment, worked in me all manner of concupiscence* (intense yearning or longing). *For without the law, sin was dead. For I was alive without the law once; but when the commandment came, sin revived, and I died. (Romans 7:6-9)*

Sufficed to say, the law which was given by God to Moses had serious shortcomings! Oh yes it did!

> *For what the law could not do, in that it was weak through the flesh, God sending His own Son in the likeness of sinful flesh, and for sin, condemned sin in the flesh; (Romans 8:3)*

The law did what it was supposed to do. It put a fence around Israel to protect that people until the Messiah, the Christ, the Chosen One would come. It never made anyone righteous, because it couldn't make anyone righteous, because it dealt with people's flesh, and flesh is never, can never, will never be righteous. Righteousness is a spiritual quality.

So the law had its Godly purpose - for a time. And during that time it caused sin to become powerfully emotionally dominant in people's lives. But there is a way out from under that dominance! The way God always intended.

> *For sin shall not have dominion over you; for you are not under the law, but under grace. (Romans 6:14)*

By simply (I didn't say "easily") submitting yourself to the grace of God, instead of to the law of Moses, sin will cease to dominate your life. Simple. Powerful. But not overnight!

How do we submit ourselves to the grace of God? You're going to have to become open to simply being an undeserving recipient of the presence (and the presents) of God and what that presence brings into your life. God will show you. If it is not coming to you as a gift, by means of and because of the work of Jesus Christ, it's not grace.

> *For by grace are you saved, through faith, and that* (faith is) *not of yourselves; it is the gift of God. (Ephesians 2:10)*

> *Now to him that works is the reward not reckoned of grace, but of debt. But to him that works not, but believes on him that justifies the ungodly* (by means of the work of His son, Jesus Christ), *his faith is reckoned for righteousness. (Romans 4:4, 5)*

Honestly, what is your mindset toward being pleasing to God? Is it your desire to please God by showing Him how much you love him by what you do? Works ! Is it your desire to dwell in His freely given loving gifts for you; to just be loved by Him; to live the gloriously fruitful life of a son and heir of all that God has and is? Grace!

Those under the law (in the flesh) are defined by what they do. Those under grace are defined by what God freely gives them through Jesus Christ.

> *That as sin has reigned unto death, so might grace reign through righteousness unto eternal life by Jesus Christ our Lord. (Romans 5:21)*

Two powerful influences in this world: By means of Satan - sin, vain endeavors. By means of Jesus Christ - grace, fruitfulness. Only one can dominate at a time. You get to choose to which of these you will yield your thoughts, your plans, your reasoning, your desires, your sense of self. Choose wisely! -.and - Plan accordingly! Choose God's generosity and expect to receive a lot of freely given gifts from God!

Being justified freely by His grace through the redemption that is in Christ Jesus; (Romans 3:24)

For Christ is the end of the law for righteousness to everyone who believes. (Romans 10:4)

THE PRIORITIES OF
A GODLY LIFE

Requirements to steady spiritual growth

The purpose of priorities is to help order our thinking, so that the will of God will come to pass in and through our lives. In football, when a quarterback goes back to pass, he does a "check-down." Receiver #1? Covered. Receiver #2? Covered. Receiver #3? Open. Boom! Pass and catch! As we have choices and decisions to make, the proper priorities will allow for Godly results.

Our priorities determine our choices and decisions, whether we are conscious of those priorities or not. Everyone's mind operates, plans, organizes, judges, and decides based on priorities. Most people's priorities are determined by a complicated series of interconnecting algorithms of which they themselves are unaware. (Since A happened, and B will probably happen, but only because of C, then I can do D, unless E gets in my way. Etc. etc. ... in this example, each letter itself stands for a complicated series of situations and circumstances, most beyond our control) I find fascinating, but not surprising, the realization that people always think they are being reasonable, even when there is no agreement concerning a specific situation between 2 or more "reasonable" people. This happens because priorities are not the same.

Every way of man is right in his own eyes; (Proverbs 21:2a)

Since every man, without Christ, is seated as god on the throne of his own life, having his perceived welfare and the need to be in control at the center of the known universe, of course every decision he makes is the correct one. Why, even when he's wrong, he's right … because his intentions were right! If our priorities come out of this consequence of eating of the tree of the knowledge of good and evil (Adam & Eve's sin), our priorities will not flow with the truth of life; and rocky, complicated, conflicted and unpredictable will be our road.

Get a Godly grasp on your priorities and you'll get a handle on a Godly life. Seriously. Allow the spirit of Christ to determine your priorities in life, and your rocky, bumpy roller coaster of a road can smooth out to a super highway of clarity and power!

1. Have the foundation laid.

For other foundation can no man lay than that which is laid, which is Jesus Christ. (I Corinthians 3:11)

The foundation is laid first. Don't even try to build anything until the foundation is laid. And there is only one, single foundation - Jesus Christ and God's love for you which is found in that very Christ. Not Jesus Christ and church membership. Not Jesus Christ and water baptism. Not Jesus Christ and good works. There is only one foundation, Jesus Christ. Everything else can burn away, but the foundation, once laid, will remain forever. (verse 15). So, the foundation is priority #1.

… For I am persuaded that … (nothing) … shall be able to separate us from the love of God, which is in Christ Jesus our Lord. (Romans 8:38a, 39b)

You aren't born persuaded. You position yourself to allow God to persuade you! In Christ is found everything that will make you complete, fulfilled and fruitful in this life. In Christ is found God's love for you, in which all things are possible! Until you are loved by God through His gift to you of the spirit of His Son, you haven't begun your spiritual journey, because it's from out of that love that all of God's workings spring; and that love is in Christ Jesus our Lord.

Allow God to set and establish the foundation of His love for you which is found only and always in Christ.

  2. Seek the lordship of Christ.

> *But seek first the kingdom of God, and His righteousness; and all these things shall be added unto you. (Matthew 6:33)*

A very familiar verse to most of you. And what is the context? Having your physical needs met, which puts this seeking of the kingdom of God outside the theoretical. Until you can learn to trust God for your physical needs, you'll still be carrying the burden of doing it yourself. When you learn to trust Him for your physical needs, then peace, healing, spiritual deliverance, wisdom and ministry are not far behind.

Notice this verse doesn't tell you how to do the seeking. If God Himself doesn't rope you into a specific expression of seeking, it would be a great disservice to Him to allow another man to do so. Read the Bible for an hour every day? Go to a fellowship every week? Sit and meditate in the truth of Christ? Seek to specifically reach out to others? It's between you and God how you seek ... but once that priority is set, be faithful to it!

Those who grow consistently spiritually are those who have seen and set the proper spiritual priorities in life. It's not rocket science! (You don't even have to be intelligent). Just set clear priorities, and then allow those priorities to determine what and how you think and how you seek Christ.

3. Love others.

When your priorities are set properly before God: that is, your foundation is Christ, and the seeking of God's rule and righteousness (which is found only in Christ) comes first, then the expression of your life will be lined up in proper Godlike balance.

Owe no man anything, but to love one another; for he that loves another has fulfilled the law. (Romans 13:8)

"No man" includes your blood family. This one directive may be simply put, but it will not be easy to establish in your lives. Lack of this priority is why most people live very complicated lives (so much drama!) as regards relationships with others. But aren't our family or our friends supposed to come first? *No!* Loving others, in the spiritual love of Christ, should come first! This means the spirit of Christ's love is what directs our efforts and priorities, not earthly obligation.

Our debt is to love, not to please others. If our priority toward others is not love, then for sure other priorities will sneak in, and our decision making will be corrupted ... our relationships will suffer, our emotional needs will be unmet, our lack and our self dissatisfaction will mount.

Distributing to the necessity of saints; given to hospitality. (Romans 12:13)

I decided many years ago that I would be "given to hospitality." (Of course I'm not going to use verses which I still fail at!) Thus, whenever any saint wants to come for a visit, or has a need to talk to me, or simply to hang out, they are welcome. If the doorbell rings and there stands an unexpected visitor ... they are welcome in my home! And I will give them what I am able to. Because hospitality is a priority, I don't have to think about how tired I am, about how I just want to sit back and watch the football game, about how much other work I have to do, and then decide how grudging I want to be in my welcome. My priority has already made my decision for me.

Now as regards your own individual expression of your life in Christ, it needs to be a priority. Get busy with it! Are you good at encouraging people in the things of the spirit? Don't let the grass grow. Give yourself to it. Seek every opportunity! Are you good at grasping the truths of the spirit? Get busy figuring out how you can share those truths with others! Are you adept at laying out truths in an orderly, easy-to-understand format? Seek and take advantage of every opportunity to teach!

Romans 12:4-8

You get to express yourself, as the spirit of Christ works within you in that unique way that is you. And it is absolutely the will of God that you be totally involved in that unique expression. It's what you owe God! Don't wait and get approval from a book, a pastor, a holy man, a friend. Allow the deepest, most powerful, expressive thoughts from God that are unique to you to change the way you think and live. Put those thoughts and impulses to the test. Prove the working of your Father within! Don't get out ahead of this working of God within, thinking you're supposed to supply your own inspiration.

Romans 12:1-3

4. Recognize and withstand the devil in the power imparted by Christ's love.

Finally, my brethren, be strong in the Lord, and in the power of his might. Put on the whole armor of God, that you may be able to stand against the wiles of the devil. For we wrestle not against flesh and blood, but against principalities, against authorities, against the wielders of the overcoming power of the darkness of this world, against wicked spirits in the spiritual realms. (Ephesians 6:10-12)

The foundation comes first, then seeking the rule of God's love and His righteousness (which is Christ) in your own heart and life, then loving others. Finally, you get to enter into the spiritual battle (or grappling contest), where you deal directly with the enemy of God!

The Priorities of a Godly Life.

1. Receive God's love in and through Jesus Christ, the foundation of our life.

2. Seek Christ (the rule and righteousness of God's love) as our inner life.

3. Love others as the spirit of Christ uniquely inspires and equips us to love.

4. In the powerful strength of the ability of the love of Christ within, stand against the devil in the spiritual contest of life.

ON BECOMING PERFECT

"Perfection is not attainable, but if we chase perfection (Jesus Christ) we can catch excellence."

This is a quote I recently came across. I have seen this same sentiment expressed many times before; and whenever I do I get this pang of regret, because every time I read a well-meaning expression like this I know that the truth is being hidden from view.

I took the time to look up the word perfect (which is the Greek word *telios*) everywhere it is used in the New Testament (19 times). In doing so, it became quite apparent that perfection is not only attainable, but is expected and made possible by God in the here and now. In short, that we walk perfectly is God's very attainable will for our lives.

The problem lies in people's perception and understanding of perfection. They think it is some undefined (and thus always unattainable) standard of physical and/or mental effort or behavior. They cannot grasp, cannot get a picture of, perfect behavior, and so they think it cannot exist. The real challenge then is to define perfection, for until it is defined, how can we ever pursue it, much less ever attain unto it? And as in all things spiritual, it behooves us to allow God to define His own terms.

Be you therefore perfect, even as your Father Who is in heaven is perfect. (Matthew 5:48)

At the time Jesus made this statement, he was the only son of God, the only one who could refer to God as his Father. Jesus tells us where the perfection he is talking about exists ... in heaven (the spiritual realm). He is telling people that the standard of perfection is God Himself, and is telling them to be like his father, God. Either that command is impossible (like the statement in quotations at the beginning of this study indicates) or it is possible.

Here in this verse is perfection defined. Perfection is spiritual (heavenly), and God is perfection. No, rather, God as Father is perfection, and knowing that God as Father is perfection, it must be perfectly obvious that the way to become perfect is to become like God as Father; in other words, to become in being and in practice God's son.

Be you therefore followers (mimetes - imitators) of God, as dear children; (Ephesians 5:1)

You can see that the translators of the King James version of the Bible did not consider the idea that man could become like God, and so they translated mimetes as "followers" instead of "imitators" or "mimics." But this is exactly what God's Son Jesus the Christ did, what he was, why he came: To restore God's original plan concerning man, which was to make man in the image of God. (Genesis 1:26, 27)

Let this thinking be in you which was also in Christ Jesus; who, being in the form of God thought ... (Philippians 2:5, 6a)

The Christ, Jesus, was like his Father ... is like his Father even today. And how did he happen to be, or become like God?

And the word was made flesh, and dwelt among us, and we beheld his glory, the glory as of the only begotten of the Father, full of grace and truth. (John 1:14)

Jesus was fathered by God. And what was his part in "attaining" unto the perfection that was his destiny from birth? Nothing at all, apart from simply accepting it as true. It was done by God, and with the intention that Jesus, as the Christ, would be the first of many perfect children fathered by God.

For whom He (God) *did foreknow, He also did predestinate to be conformed to the image of His son, that he* (Jesus) *might be the firstborn among many brethren. (Romans 8:29)*

We who have accepted the spirit of Christ to be birthed within us, are not only thus fathered by God, but are fathered in the very image, the likeness, of the Christ who is the image of God the Father. If you consider Jesus to have been perfect, then you must also consider that you yourself are also perfectly formed in the image of God. And not by your own works, your own efforts, your own behavior, but by the choice, the will and decision and working of God Himself. Because of His generosity (grace).

Well this is all so wonderfully theoretical, this perfection which God has fathered us into, but certainly we have to do something to see this perfection manifest in our lives? Hey, God's got it covered!

For it is God who works in you both to will and to do of His good pleasure. (Philippians 2:13)

God has fathered us in the perfection of Christ, and our Father will do the work required to bring that perfection into glorious reality. For one, He has provided that certain services be provided to all the body of Christ, for the purpose of bringing about His will regarding perfection.

And he (Jesus, after he left the earth) *gave some apostles, and some prophets, and some evangelists, and some pastors and teachers* (to the body of Christ)*; For the perfecting of the saints, for the work of the ministry, for the edifying of the body of Christ. (Ephesians 4:11, 12)*

Have your heart open to what these ministries have to offer. Look for those who have been sent for a specific task (apostles), for those who see into and then declare the spiritual (prophets), for those who inspire faith (evangelists), for those who help remove that which hinders (pastors), and for those who build the understanding (teachers). God is making sure these necessary services are available to those who hunger. We become perfected as we allow the working of Christ through these men and women of God to become our own.

But it is good to be zealously affected always in a good thing, and not only when I (as a minister of Christ) *am present with you. My little children, of whom I travail in birth again until Christ be formed in you. (Galatians 4:18, 19)*

This Christ being formed in the believers is the perfecting of the saints of Ephesians 4:12. This is something that is happening now! The new birth of the spirit of Christ within is not something that merely saves us from the coming wrath, not something that only does its job after death and resurrection, but it is something that is at work within us to will and to do of God's good pleasure *now*!

And our part in it all? Want it, hunger for it, seek it, allow it to happen. God does the work, but cannot go against your will. Allow God your Father to do what He desires for you and in you and through you, and walk in the perfection of the Christ within. Be perfect as your heavenly Father is perfect.

Whom (Christ in you, the hope of glory) *we preach, warning* (exhorting) *every man, and teaching every man in all wisdom;*

> *that we may present (*help cause to stand*) every man perfect in Christ Jesus. (Colossians 1:28)*

If you have a child, think of the perfection of your child. I have a grandson who is 3. He is perfect. I wouldn't change anything about him, yet he has a lot to learn. His journey through life, and the growth he will experience as he so journeys, are all a part of his perfection. Perfection is not an arrival point, but an eternal journey. Continue to be open to the working of God your spiritual Father as He continuously invites you into the perfection of His presence.

> *Brethren, I reckon (logizomai - logically reason) not myself to have arrived, but this one thing I do, forgetting those things which are behind, and reaching forth unto those things which are before, I press toward the mark for the prize of the high calling of God in Christ Jesus. Let us therefore, as many as be perfect, be thus minded, and if anything you be otherwise minded, God shall reveal even this unto you. (Phillipians 3:13)*

And finally, here is one of my favorite verses, because it was God speaking to me from out of this verse which challenged my understanding and initiated my quest for the perfection which God says he has made me to be.

> *For by one offering he has perfected forever those who are sanctified. (Hebrews 10:14)*

Now it is up to you and to me to decide to pursue our understanding, our grasp of the perfection God has made us to be in Christ.

Other New Testament verses using the same Greek word for perfection ... *telios*.

> *Romans 12:2 ... that good and acceptable and perfect will of God*

I Corinthisns 2:6 ... we speak wisdom among them that are perfect

I Corinthians 14:20 ... in understanding be perfect (KJV says "... be men")

Ephesians 4:13 ... unto a perfect man, unto the measure of the stature of the fullness of Christ

Colossians 4:12 ... that you may stand perfect and complete in all the will of God

Hebrews 5:12 ... But strong meat (of the Word) belongs to them who are perfect

SPIRITUAL WICKEDNESS

Psychological problems have spiritual causes

THE SPIRIT OF ENVY

About 3 weeks ago I was delivered from the spirit of envy. In a moment of time, the discernment of that ugly spirit came into my consciousness, and I was freed. I was painting, actually. An apartment. I was "cutting in" with a brush over a doorway, and just like that, the spirit of envy, which I've felt the effect of most all of my life, was separated from me and I was free. I could almost "see" it leave, and in its void came this glorious joy, power and peace. Praise the Lord!

I've been a seeking believer in the Lord Jesus Christ for over 40 years! 40 years! I've taught the Bible in front of hundreds and in front of few. I've preached the gospel of God's love and the sacrifice of Jesus Christ in several different countries, and all over the United States. Many people have believed because I opened my mouth to make known the gospel. I speak in tongues, always. I've counseled hundreds of people. I've healed the sick, I've even raised the dead. I've seen my prayers answered thousands of times. Yet all this time the spirit of envy afflicted my soul.

Pride and envy, they seem to go together, and they are the working of the devil. Once you become the most important thing in your life, then no one else can be better than you. When you don't have it all, aren't completely filled, then no one else should be either. When you lack, being resourced from out of the finite resources of the world, you tend to see others in a competitive way. When they get or have what you want but you don't have, you don't want them to have it either. (Now if envy has never touched your consciousness, then the above will not make any sense to you).

Jesus was put to death because of a spirit of envy.

> *For he* (Pilate) *knew that the chief priests had delivered him* (Jesus) *for* (because of) *envy. (Mark 15:10)*

Jealousy means you'll do anything to get what you want. Envy means you don't want others to have what you don't have (or at least are not enjoying the benefit of). A spirit of envy working mightily in religious people is what instigated the death of Jesus, the Christ.

When you don't feel successful, then you view others who are confident, or successful, or even at peace, as undeserving of those attributes. You attribute your feeling of lack and/or pain to those actions or words of another which make you feel less. The spirit of envy causes yo to feel less, then says, "They are losers, they shouldn't even be alive. They suck. They're jerks in every way, and so is their family, and their friends, and their work, and anything they've every done, or said, or thought." And these aren't just thoughts, but powerful feelings and emotions. You see how envy works?

A spirit of envy works because of pride, and a spirit of envy results in murderous thoughts; and, if left unchecked, murderous actions. Read Genesis 4, the account of Cain and Abel.

> *... full of envy, murder, debate* (arguing your rightness)*, deceit, malignity ... (Romans 1:29b)*

> *Now the works of the flesh are manifest, which are these; ...*

> *Envyings, murders, .(Galatians 5:19a, 21a)*
>
> *If any man teach otherwise, and consent not to the wholesome words of our Lord Jesus Christ, and to the doctrine which is according to godliness* (true inner spiritual relationship with God … not religion, which is outward show)*; He is proud, knowing nothing, but sick about questions and arguing of words, of which comes envy, strife, railings* (lashing out at others)*, suspicion, vain constant quarreling. (I Timothy 6:3, 4)*

You might be a part of a Bible group (or any kind of group), and you have thoughts of becoming a leader, of others looking up to you as someone worthy. The spirit of envy goes to work. The one who is leader now says something to you in front of others that you interpret as being dismissive, or condescending … a slight of some kind. It might even be something he doesn't do, like not choose you for some responsibility that you thought you should have gotten. From then on that leader is a jerk, and you begin to undermine his name at every opportunity. In your mind, his name and reputation, his intents and all the work he has ever done are now tainted by this spirit of envy. From that moment on, the spirit of envy will allow no good, kind or loving thought concerning that leader to grow and bear fruit in your life.

There is much envy in religion today.

> *Some indeed preach Christ of* (because of) *envy* (the very thing that put Jesus to death!) *and strife* (arguing)*, and some also of good will. The one preach Christ of contention, not sincerely, supposing to add affliction to my bonds; (Philippians 1:15)*

Because the outward show of religion is of the flesh, those who put more emphasis on religion over godliness (the actual relationship with God) will be contentious, envious, proud. They will put others down, they will get easily offended, they will speak evil of others, gossip and whisper about the sins of others; they will argue with others over correct doctrine, they will be generally unhappy, unhealthy of mind, lack peace and have little joy.

> *But if you have bitter envying and strife in your hearts, glory not, and lie not against the truth. This wisdom descends not from above, but is earthly, sensual, devilish. For where envying and strife is, there is confusion and every evil work. (James 3:14-16)*

I spend a lot of quiet time in my work, painting, inside or out. I usually work alone, and I don't play music, because I "like the sound of my thoughts." Well, like happened the other day, wonderful things can happen in my heart and mind … but not so good things can also happen; like the working of that spirit of envy for many years. I'd be painting and all of a sudden I'd be reminded of a slight done to me 10 years previously, and just like that the spirit of envy would have me "off to the races," thinking evilly of not only the one person who "wronged me," but everyone else in that same group of friends/co-workers/co-volunteers. Before I knew it, I'd be plotting my revenge! … for something that happened 10 years ago!

That's actually what was happening when that spirit of envy was revealed to me by the spirit of Christ within. I was allowing this envy to color not only a single person, but the whole family, and group they were involved with, and then one of their children was getting married, and that envy just started to include that other family being married into, and then that other group they were involved with as well. Pretty soon, there wasn't one decent person among all 50 of them!

But thank God my thoughts were stopped, and I said, "Why are you thinking this way … you like that family." And then God said, "You're envious." And I thought, "I can't be envious, that would mean I'm not perfectly wonderful, and also I'm such a spiritually together man." And then I thought, "Could I really be envious? Me?" And then it all burst into clarity as that evil spirit was exposed, and my soul was cleansed, and I was filled with the powerful love of God! And just like that, because I accepted the revelation that it was a devil spirit afflicting my mind and thoughts and feelings, that spirit was gone.

Oh, the residue was there, but not the power. And right away (I'm still brushing over this doorway), I decided to test it out. I made myself think about these people I had just been thinking about in that envy ... and there was no envy! 10 seconds later and my mind and heart had been delivered from envy! It was so easy to love them, and care about them, and desire that God bless them in every way. Because God blessing them took nothing away from me! I have since gone back in my mind and thought of everyone and anything that was ever flavored with envy ... and the cleansing has been complete!

When we turn from being supplied by God to becoming our own source of supply (which first happened in the Garden of Eden), which is a lie because it cannot be done, we begin to dwell in lack. From that position of lack, we try to supply ourselves from what we perceive as a limited supply. This is called lust, and dwelling in this lust leads to envy.

> Do you think that the scripture says in vain, "The spirit that dwells in us lusts to envy?" (James 4:5)

If you believe that you can cause yourself to be supplied by some finite resource that will make you whole, complete and fulfilled, that is lust. And because that resource is finite, and limited, your mind will compete with others for it. And when you continue to not have that fulfillment, you will look at others and think they do have it, and in this way envy can enter in and afflict your soul. This is the work of the devil, our enemy. This is not you.

You are saved by Christ, through whom we have the promise of a limitless supply of that which alone can fulfill our lives and make us whole.

But my God shall supply all your needs according to His riches in glory by Christ Jesus. (Philippians 4:19)

Now unto Him who is able to do exceeding abundantly above all that we ask or think, according to the power that works in us, (Ephesians 3:19:20)

And God is able to make all grace (generosity) *abound toward you; that you, always having all sufficiency in all things, may abound to every good work; (II Corinthians 9:8)*

The thief comes not but for to steal, and to kill, and to destroy; I am come that they (who believe on me) *might have life, and that they might have it more abundantly. (John 10:10)*

Walk away from envy. It is a working of Satan. Walk away from being your own sufficiency. Humble yourself to God, the Father of Jesus Christ, and he will fill you, supply you and lift you up in your own heart and mind, so that you have no need of envy, but instead will experience an abundance above and beyond your need, so that your desire is to share of that abundance with others. Praise the Lord!

Some examples of what might set off envy:

On the road: They cut in front of you. They beat the light, you didn't. You sat at the red light in the right lane, having to wait. Then, just as the light turns green, someone zooms by in the empty left lane.

At work: She got a promotion, even though she started after you. In a meeting, someone shares a good idea that you'd had but didn't share. You come in extra early, figuring to impress the boss … a co-worker is already there. Your boss compliments someone next to you.

At play: Someone else's kid scores a goal, when they could have passed it to your kid. All the kids in another family are naturally better athletes. You try so hard but don't do as well as someone else. Your efforts are not recognized.

In the family: Favoritism shown to anyone else but you. Good happens to them, but not so much to you. A sibling is better educated, has a better job, house, car, family, kids, etc.

In truth, all the things of God are available to you, through Jesus Christ. No one, no person, not a single soul, can stop you from receiving all the good that God desires for you to have.

WHY STRESS

And let the peace of God rule in your hearts, to the which also you are called in one body; and be thankful. (Colossians 3:15)

In order to let the peace of God rule your heart and to live without stress, it is necessary to understand that this present life is like a storm which will rage against you until you die, or until Christ returns. There exists no other successful way out of the storm other than the peace of God, because we each and every one of us has an active personal enemy who desires our extreme demise!

This is why, unfortunately, many choose to end their lives ... to escape the storm.

But there is a different way. Following are 4 helpful truths which will do battle with stress and help bring you into God's peace.

1) Be slow to fortify or justify your mental position.

Most people build shelters against the storm. They take positions in their minds and hearts which they then must defend against the attacks which come. They defend their positions with brittle, short-sighted, defective mental assertions, where they themselves are the deciders/judges of what is true and what is just. When the storms of life attack, as they do on a regular basis, the weakness and inability of these mental fortifications allows for extreme stress, where the very survival of this way of living stands in doubt at any given moment.

No wonder stress kills people. In their minds, they are "fighting for their lives," (where in reality it is only their mental position which is in danger of destruction) and the mind and body can do that for only so long before it begins to break down.

> *For I say, through the grace given unto me, to every man that is among you, not to think more highly than he ought to think; but to think soberly, according as God has dealt to every man the measure of faith. (Romans 12:3)*

Before God, we are only responsible for what we have been given by Him. Do not think you need to be better than you really are … just live in the understanding you've been supplied by God! That's enough!

> *Casting down logical reasonings and every high thing that exalts itself against the knowing of God, and bringing every thought captive unto the obedience of Christ. (II Corinthians 10:5)*

Did you ever see the movie Forrest Gump? Forrest and Lieutenant Dan were on their shrimp boat in the middle of the hurricane, and their boat made it through the storm, while all the others, which were anchored or moored in fixed positions were destroyed.

1) Be slow to fortify or justify your mental position.

2) Live off your spiritual ability, not your predeterminations.

I was in a karate tournament (taekwando to be specific). I was a red stripe belt, but sparring against black belts. I stood facing a big, brawny biker-type black belt, who I'd seen fight and even advance to the grand championships before I ever started the martial arts. Back then, I remember thinking, "Holy cats, I would never want to fight that dude!" And now I was going to be sparring him. I stood still, waiting for the fight to begin, deciding, "If he does this, then I'll do that. If he does that, then I'll do this." The referee signaled the start of the fight, and this black belt advanced on me and side-kicked me right in the chest … without me making a single move!

That's what trying to figure everything out ahead of time will do to you. It will freeze you into inaction, or poor action at best. In the above example, after getting kicked so easily, I threw away all predeterminations, and decided I would just do the best I could … and I won the match! In life there is a flow, a timing, a rhythm, and the spirit of Christ within you has the proper rhythm! Trust it.

I can do all things through Christ who strengthens me. (Philippians 4:13)

2) Live off your inner spiritual abilities, not your predeterminations. (Keep growing in your abilities!)

3) Distinguish between the work you can do and the results you desire.

The carpenter who built my house had nothing to do with the family I was able to raise in that house which he built. Often we take action, and then try to determine the results of our actions.

For example. I see my daughter engaged in self-destructive behavior. I determine to approach her and share my observations with her. Fine. But then, when I see that she doesn't respond like I think she should to my advice, I begin to nag her into heeding my advice. She becomes hostile toward me, and our relationship worsens.

My job is to share with her my observations/counsel/advice, as the spirit of God's love leads me. From there on, it is between her and God. I cannot control her life, neither will that ever be my job.

I can do what I can do, but the results need to be of God Himself.

> *And such trust have we through Christ toward God: Not that we are sufficient of ourselves to think anything as of ourselves; but our sufficiency is of God. (II Corinthians 3:4, 5)*

3) Distinguish between the work you can do and the results you desire. (Your life is yours alone to live, as are the lives of those you love).

4) Stop being the center of the universe. That's God's job.

Life existed before you were born, and it will continue after you die, should that happen before Christ returns. The world does not depend upon you for its existence, and you really need to realize this truth.

So you blew it. So what!? Pick yourself up, dust yourself off, and continue on. Learn in your doing, and be thankful for the life that's been given you to partake of. Your perfection is not a requirement for the world to continue, or even for you to live a full, rich, rewarding life, so stop trying to make existence revolve around you.

All your desires are only just that ... your desires. The world is not better when your desires are fulfilled, neither is the world worse if your desires are not fulfilled. If you are sad and lonely, the universe continues to expand as it ever did. You are not the beginner and continuer of life. You are not the arbiter of truth. You are a partaker in life. Get the most out of it by partaking. Give what you have, and enjoy what life sends your way.

> *Humble yourselves therefore under the mighty hand of God, that He may exalt you in due time. (I Peter 5:6)*

4) Stop being the center of the universe. That's God's job. (Fleshly perfection and/or carnal satisfaction is not required

for a full life).

So here have been presented 4 things which cause stress in our lives, and what we can do to be free of that stress.

1. Don't live from out of fixed fortified positions of the mind.

2. Live in the now, trusting in the ability of Christ in you.

3. Don't confuse the results you want with the work you can do. Let God produce the results. You do the work.

4. You are not the center of all that is. God is.

The grace of our Lord Jesus Christ be with you. Amen. (I Thessalonians 5:28)

EMOTIONS OF SIN

For when we were in the flesh, the motions (pathos - emotions, passions) of sins, which were by (dia - by means of) the law, did work in our members to bring forth fruit unto death. (Romans 7:5)

I'm going to give you a list of emotions, and you tell me which belong to sin.

Love ... fear ... depression .. joy ... peace ... contentedness ... anger ... jealousy ... envy ... resentment ... self-righteousness ... patience ... kindness ... tenderness ... defensiveness ... obstinateness ... pride ... maliciousness ... spite ... hate ... meekness (willingness to learn) ... humility (willingness to subject oneself) ... guilt ... shame.

There, why don't you mentally circle the ones you think are under the ownership of, or which were generated by, sin.

When you're finished reading and really understanding the truth of this study, you will begin to stop allowing certain emotions to rule or direct your life, your actions and your relationships. Instead of simply accepting these emotions as being true, and as having a right in your life and mind, you'll begin to start dealing with them as unwelcome visitors. Jesus Christ has given you the power over sin and its emotions!

In the above verse, the word "sin" is in the genitive, meaning it shows possession and/or origin. Sin generates certain emotions, and "owns" them. These emotions belong to sin, because they came from sin. That's what God says here in this verse. Of course sin itself cannot have emotions, so this must be a figure of speech, personification, meaning a giving of human qualities or traits to that which is inanimate or non-human. What this figure of speech is really saying, with particular emphasis, is that (at least some) sins which dwell in our flesh can cause us to have sinful emotions.

God also explains in this verse what causes these emotions of sin. The causer of sin's emotions is the law, speaking of the Mosaic law, of which there are 100's and not just 10. Now what the Mosaic law was to Israel, your own culture's mores and laws are to you. This is why we whisper in Church, pray before a meal, say please and thank you, apologize to others so often, etc. These laws and mores are continually telling us how we ought to behave, how we ought to think. Because (and to the degree) they are not of God, they can leave us open to or even cause sinful emotions in us – pride, arrogance, depression, anger, strife, wrath, offense, etc.

For example, I go to church, and a new family walks in, talking loudly. Upon hearing these loud voices in my usually quiet church, I might get angry at them. "Who do they think they are!" Speaking of this very law, God says in Romans 8 that this law was weak, because it dealt with our flesh which is weak, being unable to bring about Godly results.

> For what the law could not do in that it was weak through the
> flesh, … (Romans 8:3)

Now the verb "did work" back in Romans 7:5 is in the middle voice, meaning it is neither active (doing the action) nor passive (having the action done to it). Rather, this could be translated "was at work". These emotions of sin were at work in us. I'll let you guess what authority or force was the active agent causing these sinful emotions to be at work in us. (Hint: it begins with "d" and ends with "evil").

"Members" is a euphemism for the various aspects of our mind and psyche. Parts of our minds plan, reason, organize, feel, rationalize, emphasize, prioritize, decide, believe. And sins' emotions are able to work in every single one of these "members," or parts, of our minds and beings.

"To bring forth fruit" is *eis karpophoresai*, literally "the immediate result being the bringing forth of fruit." Notice the separate preposition *eis*.

"To death" is interesting, because there is not a separate Greek preposition here, like you might think there would be, as in the previous phrase. These emotions don't work in our minds to bring forth fruit with the immediate result being death. Rather, this noun, "death" is in the dative case, which indicates the person, place or thing toward which or for which the action is directed. This means that the fruit which is produced by the emotions of sins which are at work in our minds is produced for the benefit of, or is directed toward, death.

Sin generates its emotions by means of, or because of, walking in our flesh under the law (thou shalt, thou shalt not), which produces fruit, or results, directed toward death.

Sinful emotions produce fruit, and who benefits from this fruit so produced? Death!

So here's an expanded version of Romans 7:5, based on the research covered so far.

For when we were living by what we could perceive and

understand with our mind which deals with the flesh, sin's strong emotions and passions, caused by means of the law which deals with our (and others') flesh, were at work in every aspect of our mind and conscious being, unto the end of producing results which benefit only death. (Romans 7:5)

What a great picture of the vanity, darkness, and profitlessness of sin's emotions! Only death benefits from shame, guilt, anger, depression, fear, pride, etc.

But God does not leave us in this ugly state of affairs, The verse before says,

Wherefore, my brethren, you also are become dead to the law by the body of Christ; that you should be married to another, even to him who is raised from the dead, that we should bring forth fruit unto God. (Romans 7:4)

And the verse after:

But now we are delivered (rendered useless, void) *from the law, that being dead* (having died) *wherein we were held; that we should serve in newness of spirit, and not in the oldness of the letter. (Romans 7:6)*

When, in Christ, we died to the law, the law could no longer deal with the new us. Our new man is rendered useless to the law. I love this picture. The law still exists, but has nothing to do with the new, spiritual man, which is not fleshly. It would be like taking the 18th century laws of England which dealt with horses and carriages as a means of transportation and trying to apply them to the driving of cars today ... though both are means of transportation, the one has nothing to do with the other.

The law which deals with control or modification of our fleshly behavior has nothing to do with the new, spiritual beings we become once we believe unto Jesus Christ. But ask 10 Christians if they obey the 10 Commandments and 9.8 will immediately respond, "Of course I do," usually adding, "at least I try to."

The old man is not the new creation, and the laws which deal with the old man do not deal with the new creation, Christ in us.

In that new man, which is Christ in us, there are no emotions of sin at work in our minds, busily producing fruit which benefits only death. Rather, in Christ, there is only life and peace, love and fullness of joy.

> *For to be carnally minded is death; but to be spiritually minded is life and peace. (Romans 8:6)*

Let the spirit of Christ be the "judge" of all our emotions. If the emotions we have are benefiting our lives, our peacefulness, strengthening us with the ability to love, then by all means we should allow them to work within, and they will produce life-giving fruit, or results. But if the emotions which are working within us are benefiting only death, then reject them as no longer valid in our lives, having been dealt with by the death and resurrection of Jesus Christ.

We have been rendered ineffective to the law, so that sin's emotions no longer have a valid place in our minds and hearts and beings. Rather, we give place to the Lord Jesus Christ and the spirit he gave us when we first believed unto him; and as we do, our lives and every aspect of our minds and beings will abound with all manner of peaceful, enjoyable emotions and results.

> *But the fruit of the spirit is love, joy, peace, longsuffering, kindness, goodness, faith, meekness, temperance; with such no law applies itself. (Galatians 5:22, 23)*

BEWARE OF DOGS

Rejoice in the Lord and watch out for dogs.

Philippians 3:1-14

> *Finally* (to sum it all up) *my brethren, rejoice in the Lord. To write the same things to you, to me indeed is not grievous* (tedious)*, but for you it is safe. (Verse 1)*

> *Your words were found and I did eat them, and your Word was unto me the joy and rejoicing of my heart. (Jeremiah 15:16a)*

If someone is speaking the Word to you, or otherwise endeavoring to communicate to you the will of God, and it does not bring joy, or the promise of joy ... it cannot be God speaking! I'm reminded of the story a Christian brother shares about how God spoke audibly to him one day, telling him he was being "mouthy and haughty," and the result in this man's heart was pure joy!

Paul never tired of sharing and re-sharing this truth of Christ; that God wants our joy. This word "safe" is like shelter from the storm, like building our house on a rock, like having a lightning rod on the roof. We need to hear over and over and over again how God wants to serve us; how He desires our joy, our peace; how He desires our benefit. His desire is not to give us what we deserve, but rather to give to us what we need in order to live the glorious life He has designed for us.

> *Beware of dogs, beware of evil workers, beware of the concision. (Verse 2)*

Beware of dogs, those who serve only their own carnal desires. Self-serving, vain ... will be nice to you as long as it suits their selfish purpose ... will tear you to pieces if they feel threatened. Fools they are ... whatever enters into their minds they do ... they are the centers of their own universe. They use people for their own ends. Hypocrites, always trying to wear the right mask, continually seeking the approval of men.

Beware of evil workers .... they don't serve their own selfishness, they serve evil. They are con men, taken with their own cleverness Their intent is to bring evil. Difficult for us to understand, how someone would desire evil. Guess whose children they are? Satan's! They hate, despise, have no compassion. Sociopaths, psychopaths.

Beware of the concision. Refers to those Jews (and Jewish-practicing Gentiles) in the flesh, and so, religion in general. "Concision" is self-mutilation," referring to circumcision in a derogatory manner. Referring to those whose identity is in the circumcision of their flesh. We are to watch out for those whose identity is in their religion and not in Christ. Yes, perhaps especially those Christians who do not have a relationship with Jesus Christ ... Christians in name and religion only.

"Beware" is the Greek word *blepo*, (one of the words translated "to see,"). It means to use one's perceptive power of the mind. We are to keep our "eyes" open so that we recognize dogs, evil workers, and religious zealots. When we see them coming, recognizing who and what they are, we will be protected from the evil they bring. If I know someone is a con man, I won't be tricked into giving him money. If I know someone is in religious bondage, I won't get into an argument with him, or pay attention to his dogmatic rants. If I know someone is a worker of evil, I will stay away from being around him at all!

Notice that all 3 phrases start with the word Beware! He says it 3 times! This is to emphasize that each category of individual carries its own unique danger to beware of!

> *For we are the circumcision, who worship God in the spirit, and rejoice in Christ Jesus, and have no confidence in the flesh. (Verse 3)*

Note the figure of speech, *polysyndeton* (many "ands"). Each item is of equal importance.

We are the circumcision of God ... those in whom God is in the process of cutting away the evils of our dead flesh, having created a new spirit within us ... the spirit of the living Christ!! And we ....

Worship God in the spirit ... "in" is *kata*, meaning "according to." We worship God according to the supply and by the direction of the spirit of Christ within. To worship means to impart value, or worth. Anything you do, think or say in the spirit of Christ is true worship of God. As opposed to those "dogs" who simply pursue their carnal desires, we pursue a more valuable relationship with God.

Rejoice in Christ Jesus ... in our private lives, as well as in our home fellowships we seek Christ; we preach and teach Christ; we exalt and magnify Jesus Christ!! We don't argue doctrine, we don't search for sin, we hardly ever even confront sin (except in the most intimate, Godly part of our being). We leave that up to God ... He's already dealt with our sin, in Christ! We magnify our Lord Jesus Christ, and in doing so, we walk away from our sin and into the presence of God. As opposed to those who serve evil, we serve the spirit of our Lord Jesus Christ.

Have no confidence in the flesh. Amen. People spend too much time trying not to sin. It never works! In John 15, Jesus didn't say, "Try not to sin and I'll be pleased with you." He said, Abide in me and you'll bear much fruit, for without me you can do nothing (for God). As opposed to those who seek a godliness in their fleshly mind and behavior, we lay our fleshly aspirations down at the cross of Christ, having decided to stop trying to make our flesh more spiritual.

Do you want to have a closer walk with God? Then give up. Stop trying to do it yourself. Just invite God in. Look at Jesus Christ and next thing you know you'll be in the presence of God Himself, walking in His joy, peace, love and triumph!

> *Though I might also have confidence in the flesh. If any other man thinks that he has something in the flesh to trust in, I more; Circumcised the eighth day, of the lineage of Israel, of the tribe of Benjamin* (most beloved of all tribes), *a Hebrew of the Hebrews* (and yet he became the apostle to the Gentiles), *as touching the law, a Pharisee; Concerning zeal, persecuting the church, touching the righteousness which is in the law, blameless. (Verses 4-6)*

Paul was of a wealthy family. He and his family had Roman citizenship, a valuable commodity at that time. Paul was sent all the way from what is present day south-central Turkey to Jerusalem, to study with one of the greatest teachers of Jewish law of all time, Gamaliel. Paul was set for life as a Hebrew of the Hebrews. Paul was not a passive disciple of Jewish faith ... he excelled at it! He was being groomed to be a prime mover and shaker, yet ...

> *But what things were gain to me, those I counted loss for Christ. Yeah doubtless, and I count all things loss for the excellency of the experiential knowing of Christ Jesus my Lord; for whom I have suffered the loss of all things, and do count them dung, that*

I may gain Christ, And be found in him, not having my own righteousness, which is of the law, but that which is through the faith of Christ, the righteousness which is of God by faith. That I may know him, and the power of his resurrection, and the fellowship of his sufferings, being made comfortable unto his death; If by any means I might attain unto the resurrection of the dead. (Verses 7-11)

He walked away from it all. He gave up everything that exalted his identity and invited his Lord, Jesus the Christ, to take command in his life ... to express his (Christ's) life through him (Paul).

Verse 8 & 10, knowledge and know are the Greek word *gnosis*, meaning a relational, experiential knowing. Like I know my wife, my children. Like I know house painting. Paul didn't just know *about* Jesus Christ ... he literally knew him! And to grow in that relationship with Christ, Paul gave up having any other life, any other ego or pride in his own abilities, any other fleshly pursuit with worshipful intent. This was not a hardship for Paul. Paul wanted the good stuff; and, having discovered what his relationship with Christ did in and for him, he wanted all he could get!

fellowship of his sufferings ... to be able to relate to Christ in what he endured; to bring sanity and godliness into a world of insanity and godlessness. This "suffering" is the suffering of a marathon runner in training. You endure the painfully intense aspects of your training in order to compete and win.

being made conformable unto his death ... the world held nothing for him. You cannot understand this by your fleshly mind. Only as the spirit of Christ comes fully alive in you will you begin to know what this phrase means.

Not as though I had already attained, either were already perfect, but I follow after (pursue)*, if that I may apprehend that for which also I am apprehended of Christ Jesus. Brethren,*

> *I count not myself to have apprehended; but this one thing I do,*
> *forgetting those things which are behind, and reaching forth*
> *unto those things which are before, (Verses 12, 13)*

Attain and apprehend are both the same word *lambano*, meaning to lay hold of. Paul never got to the point in his experience of Christ that he figured he'd "arrived." Life as a son of God is a journey, an unending journey of spiritual delight. In fact, you've arrived when you know you're on the journey!

> *Brethren, I count not myself to have apprehended; but this*
> *one thing I do, forgetting those things which are behind, and*
> *reaching forth unto those things which are before, I press toward*
> *the mark for the prize of the high calling of God in Christ Jesus.*
> *(Verses 13, 14)*

This is the lifestyle of those who seek Christ. We don't hash over the past, try to escape it, figure it out, dwell in condemnation for it, relish its lust. After learning from it, by means of revelation from God, we just forget it. Let it go. Because we're too busy reaching forth (literally "stretching") toward what lies ahead—the high calling of God in Christ Jesus. It's just that good!

So, in summary, the reality of Christ Jesus, Lord of all heaven and earth, lies within, beckoning you forward into a greater richness and intensity of life and living. Go for it! ... but keep a watch out for dogs along the way!

RIGHTEOUSNESS

belongs wherever it is, balanced, right, working properly

THE GIFT OF GOD'S RIGHTEOUSNESS

God's Righteousness is Our Righteousness

Righteousness is defined thusly: The status of being in the right. Regarding presence, behavior, membership, plans, desires, wants, needs; all requirements are fulfilled and all is in balance.

The righteousness of God is defined thusly: The nature of God in being right in whatever He does, thinks, or plans, and in wherever He goes.

If you have the righteousness of God, then you have the rights of God.

> *Blessed are they who do hunger and thirst after righteousness; for they shall be filled. (Matthew 5:6)*

Are you 5 gallons thirsty? You'll be filled. Are you a teacup thirsty? You'll be filled. Are you an ocean thirsty? You'll be filled. Are you a universe thirsty? You'll be filled. Do you desire the rightness of being? You'll be filled. By and in and through Jesus Christ!

> *For I am not ashamed of the gospel of Christ; for it is the power of God unto salvation to every one who believes; to the Jew first,*

and also to the Greek. For therein (in the good message of Christ) *is the righteousness of God revealed from faith to faith; as it is written, The just shall live by faith. (Romans 1:16, 17)*

The word "just" in verse 17 is the root word of the word righteousness.

Righteousness - the right you have of being who you are, where you are, and doing what you're doing.

Before Adam & Eve sinned, they had no other knowledge than a simple knowing, and an experience of all the good things God had provided for them. Experiencing one another; simple, rewarding labor; provision; enjoyment of life. Life was literally a garden of experience. But when they chose to eat of the tree of the knowing of good and evil, here's what happened.

> *And the eyes of them both were opened, and they knew that they were naked; and they sewed fig leaves together, and made themselves aprons. And they heard the voice of the Lord God walking in the garden in the cool of the day; and Adam and his wife hid themselves from the presence of the Lord God among the trees of the garden. And the Lord God called unto Adam, and said unto him, Where are you? And he said, I heard your voice in the garden, and I was afraid, because I was naked, and I hid myself. (Genesis 3:7-10)*

So, lose your righteousness, and the first thing that happens is a sense of lack, of not belonging, of being out of place and in the wrong, of life being out of balance, of being naked and unprotected.

Ever walk into a room full of people that you don't know, and the volume level drops down, and everyone seems to stop what they're doing and look at you? And you are frozen in fear with the thought … I don't belong! Then you know what Adam felt that day in the garden. And, as a matter of fact, he didn't belong, and God drove him out of the garden.

By the way, because God has established His very own righteousness in me, and in the process of doing that very thing; when I walk into a room of people like in the above example, and everyone stops and looks at me, I choose to (good-naturedly) think, "Well, I know *I* belong, but I'm not sure about any of you !" (I don't say this, but I do very strongly assert this in my mind and heart).

> *For He* (God) *has made him* (Jesus Christ) *to be sin for us; who knew no sin, that we might be made the righteousness of God in him. (II Corinthians 5:21)*

This re-establishment of our righteousness was instigated by God, a long time before we were ever born.

> *Therefore by the deeds of the law there shall no flesh be justified in His* (God's) *sight; for by the law is the knowing of sin. But now* (today) *the righteousness of God without* (apart from) *the law is manifested, being witnessed by the law and the prophets; Even the righteousness of God, by faith of Jesus Christ unto all and upon all them that believe; for there is no difference* (between Jew & Gentile)*; For all have sinned, and come short of the glory of God; Being justified freely by his grace through the redemption that is in Christ Jesus; Whom God has set forth a propitiation* (repaid and restored) *through faith in his blood, to declare his righteousness for the remission of sins that are past, through the forbearance of God; To declare, at this time, His righteousness; that He might be just, and the justifier of him who believes in Jesus. (Romans 3:20-26)*

Oh please read these verses slowly, and again and again. What you do has nothing to do with your righteousness! That isn't how I was raised, probably not how you were raised. Growing up, our rightness had everything to do with how we behaved, and how we behaved never seemed to be good enough, did it?

Here, God is saying that what Jesus did is enough. And what Jesus did is enough for everyone who believes on what God did in Christ for us. Believe that. Jesus is enough. Christ is all you need, and you are absolutely, positively, wonderfully, eternally right before God!

Knowing you are right before God keeps you from being stolen from. If you find yourself in a place you don't think you belong, you'll be open and susceptible to whatever anyone says or does; including lying to you and stealing from you.

When I grew up, my family belonged to the city Country Club. They had a world class 18 - hole golf course, and on certain days we teenagers could golf. I remember one day I and my friend, Michael, who's family also belonged to the club, were just set to tee off on the first hole, when a party of 4 adult men came up to the tee, and told us to get away from there, because they were about to golf. Well, I was old enough, and bold enough, that I looked at them and said, "Sorry, but we have a right to be here, and you guys have to wait for us." And we went right ahead and golfed, and those 4 men waited for us. I asserted my right, and there was nothing they could do.

You have rights before God, in Christ. First of all, you have the right to be. That is huge! Become rooted in the righteousness of Christ within. In Christ, you have the same rights as God Himself.

In Christ, you have the right to act. To make mistakes and try again. Yes! The right to try again. The right to hold your head up high in the presence of God, as well as in the presence of God's enemies. That includes Satan, and all the unbelievers in the world.

So, where does the idea of "Watch your witness" come from? (Watch how you act in front of unbelievers). Not from God, that's for sure. It's one of Satan's lies, meant to steal away from you the gift of your righteousness - your right standing before God.

When Christ was being tortured and killed, do you think he hung his head in shame? No. He held his head up high, for he was the righteousness of God.

> *But of him* (God) *are you in Christ Jesus, who from God is made unto us wisdom, and righteousness, and sanctification, and redemption; (I Corinthians 1:30)*

The new creation (that which each one of us is, in Christ) was created by God Himself. And every work of God is righteous, because God is righteous.

> *And that you put on the new man, which after God is created in righteousness and true holiness. (Ephesians 4:24)*

> *For what the law could not do, in that it was weak through the flesh, God sending His own son in the likeness of sinful flesh, and for sin, condemned sin in the flesh; That the righteousness of the law might be fulfilled in us, who walk not after* (resourced by) *the flesh, but* (resourced by) *the spirit* (of Christ). *(Romans 8:3, 4)*

In and because of the work of Christ Jesus our Lord, we have been made into the quality of righteousness itself, for we are the nature of God himself. As such, we have the rights of God Himself. We are born out of God Himself. All this work was instigated and is carried out by God Himself, through His son Jesus Christ.

It is on the foundation of our righteousness before God that God is free to bestow all his good generosity upon us, and through us toward others.

> *That as sin has reigned unto death, even so might grace reign through righteousness unto eternal life by* (means of) *Jesus Christ our Lord. (Romans 5:21)*

Jesus Christ is our righteousness. Forget trying to do it yourself, trying to be good enough in the eyes of God. Rather, humble yourself before God and accept this glorious truth, that God has given you His very own nature. Righteousness. As a gift! You have God's right to be. You have God's right to do. You have God's right to do, and then do again!

THE APPROVAL OF MAN

Approval is important.

And when they had brought them, they set them before the council; and the high priest asked them, Saying, Did not we adamantly command you that you should not teach in this name? and behold, you have filled Jerusalem with your doctrine, and intend to bring this man's blood upon us (well, they *did* have him crucified!). *Then Peter and the apostles responded and said, We ought to obey God rather than men.* (Acts 5:27-29)

We all need approval. Approval lets us know we're doing something right, going in the right direction (as far as the one doing the approving is concerned). We've all grown up seeking the approval of man. First, our parents; then perhaps our siblings, teachers, friends; then, bosses, co-workers, others we look up to or whose authority influences our lives. Unless and until we learn how to get God's approval, we'll continue to need man's approval.

Approval affects self image, sense of worth, happiness, self-confidence, fruitfulness, accomplishment, quality of life, peacefulness, righteousness, self-esteem, ability to love others. Without approval there lurks depression, anger, resentment, rebellion, shame, confusion. By seeking approval in the wrong ways, or from the wrong sources, there results lust, drunkenness, revelry (partying hard), strife (arguing), harsh judgmentalism, sexual perversions of every sort.

No matter how hard we seek after it, the approval of man cannot fulfill us. It cannot make us complete. It cannot fill up our need for approval. For these things to come about we need to mature and grow into beings who stand approved before God rather than man.

In the Christian sphere I have heard of accountability partners. A person, or people, with whom you get together on a regular basis in order to "answer to them;" to be "held accountable." This supposedly helps a person stay away from sin, with the purpose of growing closer to God.

But in truth, the need to stand approved before man hinders our spiritual growth. It keeps us weak and unable to bear fruit. It keeps the door open to Satanic attacks of all kinds. When Pastor Such-and-Such, or the Right Reverend So-and-So has to like what we're doing, has to put his/her stamp of approval on our spiritual endeavor, we will live very anemic spiritual lives.

So what does the Word of God have to say about being accountable to another man, no matter how well-intentioned?

> *For do I now persuade men, or God? or do I seek to please men?*
> *For if I yet pleased men, I would not be the servant of Christ.*
> *(Galatians 1:10)*

First, let's define accountability. It's needing to answer to someone. It's allowing yourself to be defined by their judgment. It's not the same as being subject to someone. Subjection is always voluntary, but accountability speaks of demanded judgment. If you are accountable to me, then I will decide if and when you have done something correctly, or done enough, or done too much. I will decide if you're even going in the right direction! This way of living never produces powerful, free, fruitful Christians.

On the other hand, if you subject yourself to my ministry (not me, but my ministry in Christ), then you position yourself to receive the spirit of Christ which works through me. However, you are never to be accountable to me, to answer to me. You are accountable to Christ alone!!!

> *Let every soul be subject onto the higher powers, for there is no power but of God. The powers that be are ordained of God. Whosoever therefore resists the power resists the ordinance of God; and they who resist shall receive to themselves damnation* (judgment). *(Romans 13:1)*

These are spiritual authorities in the church (the body of Christ). These "higher powers" is a single Greek word, exousia, and means "authority," which is the way it is often translated in the Bible. Let every soul be subject unto the authorities. The word "ordained" means prepared. This authority is of God, thus it is speaking of spiritual authority and not civil authority, as is so often understood and even translated.

We subject ourselves to the authority, not to the man or woman evidencing that authority. Since Christ is the spiritual authority, these authorities are his authorities. If we subject ourselves to Christ's authority working in and through others, we are putting ourselves under Christ's authority, not under that man or woman.

On the other hand, if we subject ourselves to the man (or woman) who happens to evidence Christ in a dynamic way, then we will be led astray when he (or she) goes astray. This happens quite often in the evangelical, organized church.

> *Let no man beguile you of your reward in a voluntary humility and worshiping of angels, intruding into those things which*

he has not seen, vainly puffed up by his fleshly mind, and not holding the head, from which all the body by joints and bands having nourishment ministered, and knit together, increases with the increase of God. (Colossians 2:18, 19)

Here we are admonished by God Himself to not hold ourselves accountable to another man, but rather to adhere only to Christ. Hold to Christ, be nourished by Christ, do not stray from Christ.

What I see in the home fellowships of which I am or have been a part is a subjection to Christ, no matter who he works in at the moment. When someone shares Christ working in them we listen, we receive, we (at least seek to) understand, we are edified and blessed, we grow. But who was that person who manifested Christ?

Who then is Paul, and who is Apollos, but ministers by whom you believed, even as the Lord gave to every man? I have planted, Apollos watered; but God gave the increase. So then neither is he that plants anything, neither he that waters,; but God Who gives the increase. (I Corinthians 3:5, 6)

When, and as, and to the degree we subject ourselves - not to the man, but to the working of the spirit of Christ within that man - we will grow, be fed and watered, nourished, led in paths of righteousness. To the degree we subject ourselves to the man, we lay ourselves open to deception and lies.

Of course the organized, denominational church will not like to hear this, because their authority often is not the authority of Christ, but rather that given by man.

But though we, or an angel from heaven, preach any other gospel unto you than that which we have preached unto you, let him be accursed. As we said before, so say I now again, If any man preach any other gospel unto you than that which you have received (from Christ, through us), *let him be accursed.*

> *For do I now persuade men, or God? or do I seek to please men?*
> *For if I yet pleased men, I should not be the servant of Christ.*
> *(Galatians 1:8-10)*

This seeking to please men occurs when a person holds himself accountable to them.

Now when it speaks of being subject to fathers, mothers, husbands, wives, etc., it is referring to subjection to the authority they have in that area. In the area of the spirit, regarding obedience to and fellowship with God, Jesus Christ has all the authority!

And so, when we speak of "being accountable" to anyone other than Christ, we cannot be speaking of spiritual accountability.

> *But speaking the truth in love, may grow up into him in all*
> *things, who is the head, Christ; From whom the whole body*
> *fitly joined together and compacted by that which every joint*
> *supplies, according to the effectual working in the measure of*
> *every part, makes increase of the body unto the edifying of itself*
> *in love. (Ephesians 4:15, 16)*

We have one head, Jesus Christ. Spiritually, we are accountable only to him. He alone is Lord of heaven and earth.

> *Study to show yourself approved unto God, a workman that*
> *needs not to be ashamed, rightly dividing the word of truth.*
> *(II Timothy 2:15)*

The word "study" does not mean an academic studying; rather, it indicates an application of self to the task at hand. We are to apply ourselves, conscientiously and with diligence, to the task of standing approved unto God. No one can seek God's approval and man's approval at the same time (want both, yes; but seek both, no).

"Rightly dividing" should be understood to be a mental and

emotional undertaking, rather than an academic one. The "word of truth" does not mean simply what the Bible says, meaning the words printed on the page. We've all met people who are enamored with their knowing of what the Bible says. Rather, we seek the truth of the words. We contemplate, dwell on and seek to understand. We endeavor to walk in the light of, the truth of, what God communicates of Christ to us. Only His spirit within us can bring us into that light, because His spirit (the spirit of Christ) *is* the light.

Thus, the more we seek to stand approved before God by clear and practical understanding of God's communication of Christ within us, the less we will seek the approval of man.

> *How are you able to believe, who receive unto yourselves honor (doxa – glory) from one another, and seek not the honor (doxa) which comes from the only God? (John 5:44)*

And so the holy spirit of God frees us from seeking to please man, which never results in lasting benefit, but rather only enslaves us to the flesh. Rather, His holy spirit frees us to actually, practically stand approved before God and bear the spiritual fruit of that successful endeavor.

To conclude, I understand that there will never be, can never be, a large mass of people who all meet in a single place who will all, being led by the spirit of Christ, work in total physical harmony as man considers it harmony. This picture of unity was never drawn by the holy spirit of God, but rather is a picture of unity drawn by God's enemy, Satan, who only seeks to enslave. Christ has made us free to truly pursue and discover the true God. This can never, ever happen at the direction of a man (walking in the mind of his flesh), but can only happen by the intimate direction of God's holy spirit within, the spirit of Christ.

And though by many outward appearances there is little or no physical unity in a large group of individuals each being led by the spirit of God, there is total, uninhibited spiritual unity, as the truth of the following verse flows unto its unlimited potential ...

> *And we know that all things* (of the spirit) *work together for good to them that love God, to them who are the called according to His purpose. (Romans 8:28)*

JUSTIFIED—WHAT IT MEANS

Somebody's got to be to blame for the evil

Being justified freely by His grace through the redemption that is in Christ Jesus: (Romans 3:24)

Justified, justification are nice religious words, aren't they? We read them in the Bible, but do we know what they mean? Does our understanding of our justification change our lives, our thoughts, our psyche? Does it change the way we approach God and each other? Does it change the way we think of ourselves and our place before God?

In this study, we'll take a look at the word itself, then at its spiritual truth, then at its practical import in and for our lives.

The word for "justify" in the Greek is *dikaioo*. Related words are justification, righteous, righteousness. The root word for all of these words is *dikaios*, translated just and righteous. At its root, to be justified means to be made or to be judged as just. Let's take a look at the very first time that word is used in the New Testament.

Then Joseph her husband, being a just man, and not willing to make her a public example, was minded to put her away privately. (Matthew 1:19)

In ancient Israel, the consequence ("public example") for a newly married woman being found by her husband to have lost her virginity before they consummated their marriage could be as severe as stoning her to death in front of the door of her father's house! (Deuteronomy 22:13-29). I say "could" because it was contingent upon her new husband "hating" her, meaning he had withdrawn all feelings of affection for her, and wanted her to suffer.

So we see that behavior and consequence are totally wrapped up in this word "just." Mary was found to be pregnant before Joseph had sex with his new wife, and Joseph was just, therefore, there had to be consequence, in order to bring justice or balance to the situation. But Joseph had affectionate feelings for Mary, and didn't want to have her stoned to death. But there *had* to be consequence, so he was going to "put her away." Send her to another part of the country, if not abroad, and pretend he'd never married her.

In our culture, as well as others, the idea of justice is represented by a woman holding a set of balancing scales. And that is the root of the word justify - to bring things into moral or spiritual balance.

Here's an example of justification. I'm a house painter. A couple of weeks ago, I painted a bathroom in the home of a middle aged couple, who both worked during the day, who had recently refinished their entire kitchen, including brand new sink. That evening, after my first day on the job, the woman called me to tell me that she was angry because I'd washed my equipment in her brand new kitchen sink. It was true, I had! But, I told her, I'd asked her husband before he left for work if they had a utility sink I could use, and he'd said no, but that I could just use the kitchen sink. I was justified! It was true, I'd done it. But I was justified in doing it! The woman's anger could now be turned upon her husband!

The truth of the matter was that this couple did have a utility sink.

Maybe the man had been distracted when I asked, but the truth was that he did indeed have the authority to okay my using of the kitchen sink. My reason for using the sink justified my behavior. The argument was between the woman and the man, even though I was the "culprit." I was justified in what I did, and so did not have to pay a consequence.

So it is with sin. In Christ, we are "off the hook" of having to pay any consequence for sin, including death. (Notice I say "in Christ") The devil is, and has been judged as, responsible for all sin. We partake of that sin (we are the culprit!) but our reasons for sinning are justified in Christ, because in Christ the devil is to blame for our sin. Why then was God so "angry" with sin and sinners in the Old Testament? The same reason the woman was so angry with me before I'd been justified.

Therefore by the deeds of the law there shall no flesh be justified in His sight; for by the law is the knowledge of sin. (Romans 3:20)

This word "knowledge" is *epignosis*, meaning intimate or thorough experiential knowing. We sin, and know it's sin, due to the law saying, "Don't do that." No one's mind which deals with the flesh and having the *epignosis* of sin can be justified.

Therefore we conclude that a man is justified by faith without the deeds of the law. (Romans 3:28)

Not by doing good, neither by not doing evil, is a man justified, but by receiving unto himself the spirit of what Jesus accomplished by his death and resurrection. The spirit of the risen and glorified Christ is just, and is the justifier of all those who receive that spirit, by faith in the death and resurrection of Jesus. When we believe, we receive a new life, a justified life.

Knowing this, that our old man is crucified with him (Jesus), that the body of sin might be destroyed, that from now on we should not serve sin. For he that is dead is justified (KJV Bible incorrectly reads "freed") *from sin. (Romans 6:6, 7)*

Jesus came to save mankind, by exposing, defeating and judging the devil. You cannot have the one without the other. Man's salvation comes into living reality in his life only as and to the degree that Satan and his works are exposed as the cause of sin in his life.

The devil was defeated by the death and resurrection of Jesus Christ, exposed as the one to blame for sin. Until then, the consequences of sin (the anger, or wrath of God) provided the balance for sin. But now the balance for sin lies with the devil being judged as the guilty party, and his final punishment. The devil's guilt is found in Christ, and that is the same place our justification lies.

> *But for us also, to whom it* (righteousness) *shall be imputed, if we believe on Him who raised up Jesus our Lord from the dead; Who was delivered for our offenses, and was raised again for our justification. (Romans 4:24, 25)*

The resurrection of Jesus Christ involved the judgment of Satan as the guilty party for the sins of the whole world. In that judgment, we are absolved of all blame for sin. We are, quite literally, justified from sin. Someone has to be blamed and suffer the consequences. Praise the Lord that in the death and resurrection of Jesus Christ, we are justified and the devil is discovered, or uncovered, as the offending party, and it is the devil who will suffer the consequences for that sin for all eternity.

> *Wherefore, as by one man sin entered into the world, and death by sin; and so death passed upon all men, for that all have sinned; For if by one man's offense death reigned by one; much more they who receive abundance of grace and of the gift of righteousness shall reign in life by one, Jesus Christ; Therefore as by the offense of one judgment came upon all men to condemnation; even so by the righteousness of one the free gift*

came upon all men unto justification of life. For as by one man's disobedience many were made sinners, so by the obedience of one shall many be made righteous. (Romans 5:12, 17-19)

The spirit of the risen Christ makes known Satan as the guilty party for all the sins of the world, which is why man can justly be forgiven for them all. That is our justification, what the death and resurrection of Jesus Christ accomplished - Satan is the guilty party.

Nevertheless I tell you the truth; it is beneficial for you that I go away; for if I go not away, the Comforter will not come unto you; but if I depart, I will send him unto you. And when he is come, he will reprove the world of sin, and of righteousness, and of judgment; Of sin, because they believe not on me; Of righteousness, because I go to my Father, and you see me no more; Of judgment, because the prince of this world is judged. (John 16:7-11)

The prince of this world was not judged guilty of the sins of the world until the death and resurrection of Jesus. Until then, he stayed hidden as the guilty party, and man bore the condemnation. But now, in Christ, every man is justified from sin, the devil having been found guilty for all sin.

What are the ramifications of this justification? Rest easy, no one would choose failure over success, that which does not work over that which does work. No one would choose malice and hate over love and joy. The only reason we do is because of Satan's deception. God knows that, and Jesus proved that.

What shall we then say to these things? If God be for us, who can be against us? He that spared not His own Son, but delivered him up for us all, how shall He not by means of him also freely give us all things? Who shall lay anything to the charge of God's elect (charge God's elect with a crime worthy of punishment)? *God, who justifies? Who is he that condemns? Christ, who died,*

*yeah rather, who is risen again, who is even at the right hand
of God, who also makes intercession for us? (Romans 8:31-34)*

Do you really think that after God has gone to all the trouble of
providing a way to justify you of all sin, putting the blame and
judgment squarely on the devil, that He is now going to be in a big
hurry to club you over the head for that same sin?

Yes, we are responsible for the decisions we make, but before God
we are blameless for that which seeks to separate us from God.
Being justified freely by Jesus Christ, we can stop thinking about
guilt and blame, and start seeking the righteousness that leads us
into the blessed, fruitful life God has always intended for us all along.

According as He (God) *has chosen us in him* (Christ) *before
the foundation of the cosmos, that we should be holy and
without blame (*it doesn't say "sinless"*) before him in love.
(Ephesians 1:4)*

HOLY AND WITHOUT BLAME

According as He (God) *has chosen us in him* (Christ) *before the foundation of the cosmos, that we should be holy and without blame before Him* (God) *in love* (many translations put these last 2 words "in love" at the beginning of the next verse). *(Ephesians 1:4)*

The word "holy" is the Greek word h*agion.* It is the same word as is used in the expression "holy spirit" or "Holy Ghost." It means pure, undefiled, dedicated or set aside or set apart, not for common use. It generally has the meaning of being set aside for a specific use or purpose. The word "saints" is the plural form of this word (as in Ephesians 1:1), which should more accurately be translated "holy ones" or "those (who are) holy."

I searched the entire Old Testament and was only able to find the term "holy spirit" (whether or not it is capitalized in your version of the Bible) used 3 times - in the entire Old Testament! Psalm 51:11, Isaiah 63:11, 12, all of which deal with salvation, deliverance.

In the New Testament, this term, "holy spirit" (or "Holy Ghost") is used 27x in the Gospels, 41x in Acts (of the Apostles), 15x in Paul's general epistles (Romans-Thessalonians), 2x in Timothy and Titus, and 9x in the rest of the New Testament, not including Revelation, where it is not used at all. That's 3x in the Old Testament, 94x in the New Testament!

The nature and dedicated purpose of this holy spirit is defined/described in the following verses: (this is not in any sense an exhaustive list - there are many more).

> ... but if (when) *I depart, I will send him unto you. (John 16:7b)*

> ...*whom I will send unto you from the Father ... which proceeds from beside the Father, he shall testify of me. (John 15:26)*

> ... *whom the Father will send in my name, he shall teach you all things, and bring all things to your remembrance, whatsoever I have said unto you. (John 14:26)*

> *But whosoever drinks of the water that I shall give him shall never thirst; but the water that I shall give him shall be in him a well of water springing up into everlasting life. (John 4:14)*

> ... *He that believes on me, as the scripture has said, out of his belly shall flow rivers of living water. (But this he spoke of the spirit, which they who believe on him should receive; for the holy spirit was not yet given; because that Jesus was not yet glorified). (John 7:39)*

> *And when he is come, he will reprove (expose in and by the light of truth) the world concerning sin, and concerning righteousness, and concerning judgment; Concerning sin, because they believe not unto me; Concerning righteousness, because I go away toward my Father and you see me no more; Concerning judgment, because the ruler of this world is judged. (John 16:8-11)*

... when he, the spirit of truth, is come, he will guide you into all truth. (John 16:13)

He shall glorify me; ... (John 16:14)

... he shall take of mine, and shall show it unto you. (John 16:15)

... he shall testify of me. (John 15:26b)

This holy spirit, sent into the world by God by means of Jesus Christ, to be received into the lives of all who believe unto Jesus Christ, is not a static thing. It gives life, light, love and power to all who allow its life to bubble forth. The holy spirit of God ("Christ" means the anointing of the holy spirit) is dynamic, imparting its nature, the nature of God Himself, to everyone in whom it abides. This imparted nature is "Christ in you."

It is the holy spirit that makes us holy, not our behavior. As the holy spirit flows through us; our being, our nature is transformed into the image of God (Christ is the image of God), becoming more and more like Jesus himself. This is an inside job, not an outward show.

> *Now the Lord is that spirit, and where the spirit of the Lord is, there is liberty. But we all, with open face beholding as in a mirror the glory of the Lord, are changed into the same image from* (one) *glory to* (another) *glory* (it's all glory!), *even as by the spirit of the Lord. (II Corinthians 3:17, 18)*

> *... Christ in you, the hope of glory. (Colossians 1:27b)*

This term, "holy spirit" can be understood as "purifying spirit" in that the term "holy" refers not only to a state of being, but to a work being carried out in our lives.

> *For John truly baptized with water; but you shall be baptized in the holy* (purifying) *spirit not many days hence. (Acts 1:5)*

Washing with water (baptism) was very important in the Jewish faith, and whenever possible was to be carried out in running water, which is why John the Baptizer baptized in a river. This is so that the impurities which the water cleanses from the person or object being baptized could be carried away by that same water. So it is with the holy spirit of God not only cleansing us, but carrying our impurities away. This it does on an ongoing basis. In fact, it never sleeps, never stops; it provides what it is - an endless supply.

The holy spirit has sealed us unto a fate which overcomes death, continually delivering us into an eternal life of manifesting forth the glory of God, the Father.

> *... after you believed, you were sealed with that holy spirit of promise, Which is the down payment of our inheritance ... (Ephesians 1:13b, 14a)*

> *That we should be to the praise of His glory, ... (Ephesians 1:12)*

> *... and he that loves me shall be loved of my Father, and I will love him, and will manifest myself to him. (John 14:21b)*

The holy spirit of God is like God, continually providing life, health, wisdom, and power to and for those who draw on it by seeking Christ. The holy spirit of God is continually exposing sin in our lives as the working of the devil, thereby continually justifying us in the process, rendering us righteous. This finished working by the holy spirit of God, a gift from out of God's generosity, can never be accomplished by anything we do, other than to simply accept it as true for our lives.

The supply of the spirit of God is limitless, unbounded by the limited resources which the world is constantly throwing in our faces as truth. God, our spiritual Father, is continually calling to us to accept his unlimited spiritual supply as the established truth in our lives.

One of the worst things we can do (and Satan has been tricking us into this very thing our whole lives) is to seek to deliver ourselves from the devil's trickery by our will power to modify our thinking and behavior. This endeavor doesn't work, hasn't worked and will never work, so abandon it completely, once and for all! Stop trying to be better, or to act better, or to stop acting poorly as the means to a Godly life by your own carnal efforts. Instead, seek Christ, the generous working of the spirit of God within, which will continue to provide your mind and heart all the good things of God for your use and enjoyment.

This is why the purifying work of the holy spirit renders us without blame. The blame has been put on the devil, for all time. And because we now have access to the limitless resources of God Himself, via His spirit in us, we have no reason to blame anyone else (other than the devil) for any of the evil which touches our lives.

My wife doesn't make me angry. This traffic jam doesn't make me frustrated. My losing my job doesn't depress me. That illogical viewpoint doesn't make me argue. That emptiness is not caused by my lack or failure or shortcoming. That boredom doesn't mean I'm not doing enough. That guilt is only good for letting me know I'm not in Christ, where there is no guilt. That shame comes from the devil, not my behavior. That blame comes from my being blamed by the devil for his own devious working, because in Christ there is no blame.

Imagine a life with no blame! Any and all sin evidenced in my life is simply an area not yet reached by the limitless love of Christ. God is not blaming me for it, because He has cast all blame on the devil, where it belongs. Wherever and whenever I am touched by the deceitfulness of sin, all of which is initiated and fomented by the devil, I have no one to blame but him. I blame no other person, not even myself.

> *But with me it is a very small thing that I should be judged of you, or of man's judgment; yea, I judge not mine own self. (I Corinthians 4:3)*

We are holy (and getting holier) and without blame. We are not blamed by God, we do not carry blame, and so we do not blame others. God is continually challenging us to understand, accept and believe this as true for our lives. Of course this can not be understood or believed except by the revealing work of the holy spirit of God, the revelation of the Christ within.

> *The God of our Lord Jesus Christ, the Father of glory, may give unto you the spirit of wisdom and revelation in the intimate knowing of him* (Christ)*; The eyes of your heart being enlightened; that you may know what is the hope of his calling, and what are the riches of the glory of His inheritance in the holy ones, And what is the exceeding greatness of His power toward us who believe, ... (Ephesians 1:17-19a)*

RELIGION

What man does in reaching for his own righteousness

THE DEATH OF DOGMA

A study of Colossians 2:14-23

> *Blotting out the handwriting of ordinances that was against us,*
> *which was contrary to us, and took it out of the way, nailing it*
> *to his cross; (Verse 14)*

What the heck is this verse saying? I've heard it taught as being
similar to the truth of Isaiah 40.

> *Speak comfortably to Jerusalem, and cry unto her, that her*
> *warfare is accomplished, that her iniquity is pardoned; for she has*
> *received of the Lord's hand double for all her sins. (Isaiah 40:2)*

The custom of dealing with bankruptcy in those times is here
in Isaiah compared with God dealing with the sins of Israel. At
the entrance into a city the names and debts of those bankrupt
individuals unable to pay their debts were published, so that people
would know not to do business with them. Then if someone (say,
an old family friend) were to come along and pay off all a person's
debts, or they themselves were able to negotiate a satisfaction of
their debt, their list of debts would be "doubled," that is, folded
over to hide those debts, and marked "paid" (with the name of the

individual still visible) so that people would know that person was now free and clear of all debt.

But this is not what Colossians 2:14 is saying. To "blot out" means to smear or to plaster over. "Ordinances" is the Greek word *dogmata*, from which we get our word "dogma." Dogma is a belief not "installed" and proven in a person's life, a belief which has not yielded any fruit. Dogma is the opinion of man which carries a force as if it were a spiritual law, though it is not of God. This verse in Colossians reinforces the truth that this dogma is of man by using the word "handwriting."

Some examples (there are thousands) of dogma are: When you sing in Church you should raise your arms. We should pray before meals. Christians should vote Republican. Family first. A person who has graduated from a seminary is a man of God. We must give 10% of everything we earn to the church we belong to. We should go to church every Sunday. We should always be polite. None of these things is commanded or stated by God, at least in the New Testament. Though none of these things is written down as a commandment, (and thousands of pages have been written by man concerning these things as being needful), yet these concepts rule people's lives as if commanded by God. They carry a force of spiritual law though they are the opinions of man.

Notice I am not saying here that these things are evil. I am only saying that God has not commanded them; but rather that man has. If there has been any fruit in subjecting ourselves to any of this dogma, that fruit has come, not in obeying the dogma, but by coming into fellowship with God; by coming into Christ; by walking in the leading of His spirit within.

Now verse 14 goes on to say that this dogma of man is "against us" and is "contrary to us." This is a figure of speech, stating the same truth twice, which is meant to emphasize that this dogma is our enemy. "Against" means opposite. If I'm going up, the dogma is pulling downward. If I desire to be in, the dogma is calling me out. If I'm moving forward, the dogma is demanding I go backward. It is opposed to me and the direction and the way I want to go. "Contrary" means adversarial by stealth; that is, it acts like a friend, but is an enemy. This word "contrary" in the plural is translated "adversaries."

In Christ, God has made us free. But the devil does not want us to enjoy that freedom which is now rightfully ours, so he works in people, or even just in our minds directly, to throw up spiritual roadblocks to our freedom under the guise of rules that are beneficial to us, but which in reality keep us from realizing our full potential. All this dogma actually falls under the realm, and is a result of, eating of the fruit of the tree of the knowledge of good and evil.

Some of this dogma is self-imposed. For example, "you need to read the Bible for 15 minutes every morning before you leave for work, or God will not be able to bless you." "You need to pray for everyone you know every day lest something bad happen to someone."

God plastered over all these opinions, all this dogma. He smeared it, meaning it's clearly stated intent has been rendered illegible, powerless, unnecessary. God nailed all of this dogma to the cross of His son, so that when Jesus died, any need to conform to the forceful (and religious) opinions of man died with him. In their place the clear simple light of truth bursts forth in Christ. What was a maze of rules and regulations which introduced themselves to us as friends and helpers on the path to God but were in reality hindrances on that path, now have become dead to us, and we to them. In Christ are found no such dogmatic rules or regulations.

And having spoiled principalities and powers, He made a show of them openly, triumphing over them in it. (Verse 15)

To "spoil" is a term of warfare that indicates the taking away of anything of value. This verse is powerfully connected with the previous, indicating and exposing the powers and influences which were responsible for this dogma which sought to cozy up to us as friends, but which in truth were our enemies from the start, keeping us from coming into and walking in the presence of God.

> *Let no man therefore judge you in meat, or in drink, or in respect of a holy day, or of the new moon, or of the sabbath days; Which are a shadow of things to come; but the body is of Christ. (Verses 16, 17)*

See, the influence is devilish, but it comes so often through a man, through religion. Because the cross of Christ has buried this dogma, we have to stand against it, wherever and whenever it tries to make our flesh conform to its devilish judgments. "You really ought to go to church." "We have to respect others' opinions." "We have to keep an open mind." The real thing, Christ, has come. Why then continue to serve shadows and representations of the real thing? The devil seeks to rob us of what Christ has rightfully bought for us, by making us believe we haven't yet earned it!

> *Let no man beguile you of your reward* (defraud you by acting as an umpire) *in a voluntary humility and worshiping of angels* (messengers) (we put people on spiritual pedestals), *intruding into those things which he has not seen* (ie: the working of Christ in your life), *vainly puffed up by his fleshly mind,* (Verse 18)

Christians judge other Christians. You're good, you're bad. You shouldn't do this. You ought to be doing more of that. The judgments are endless. "We ought to" and "We should" seem to dominate the Christian landscape. But God says, "You have" and "You can" and "You only need Christ." If we accept the dogma and judgments of man, we subject ourselves to the devil and his ways, which keep us from walking in the completed work of Christ and keep us from the presence of God.

These "angels" (*angelos*) are messengers. Man has a tendency to worship the messenger. These messengers include famous Christian men and women. Some have TV shows; some have gigantic buildings which hold tens of thousands of people; many have written well known books. These messengers are not evil; the evil lies in worshiping them. We can be thankful for them, hold them in high regard, but realize they are men who need Christ just like we do.

> *And not holding the head, from whom all the body by joints and bands having nourishment ministered, and knit together, increases with the increase of God. (Verse 19)*

Rather, hold to the head, Christ. Never let any influence, rule, dogma, opinion, man or spirit get in the way between you and Christ. Christ is not the most important thing, he is the only thing. We grow into Godly beings by being nourished by the spirit of Christ. If we are not in Christ, we can not be nourished by him. He is the answer to all our needs, all our questions, all our desires, all our purposes. In Christ we are completely complete, fully realized, wholly individual. In Christ we become completely, uniquely, powerfully ourselves! Don't let anything or anyone get between you and Christ.

> *Wherefore if you be dead with Christ from the rudiments of the world, why, as though living in the world, are you subject to ordinances (Touch not; taste not; handle not; Which all are to perish with the using;) after the injunctions and teachings of man? (Verses 20-22)*

What dogma influences your life? What religious beliefs do you hold true that are not taught by the rightly divided Word of God (that which is addressed to you and to be believed and applied by you who are saved by grace today)? What opinions of man carry the force of law in your life and heart? What beliefs do you hold powerfully to that have failed to ever produce spiritual fruit in your life? You keep them, it feels like, simply to stave off the wrath of God. They have acted as friends, but have been your enemy, keeping you from enjoying your life in Christ. If you can identify them, you can stand against them, turn your back on them and freely cling to Christ where before you could not. Do not be afraid to be different, to be "other than" the vast herd of conforming Christianity. Come completely into your own and be the glorious individual God has called you to be and Christ enables you to be.

> *Which things* (injunctions and teachings of man) *have indeed a show of wisdom in will worship and humility, and neglecting of the body; not in any honor to the satisfying of the flesh. (Verse 23)*

Forget trying to argue with these influences, you can not win. Simply hold them up to the light of Christ. Either they are of Christ or they are not. And then choose Christ, and let his spirit deal with all this adversarial dogma, the need for which has died on the cross with Christ.

SPIRITUAL PINBALL

I was recently reading a past study from www.givemechrist.com, Freedom in Christ, and I was thinking about how powerful is that truth of our freedom in Christ. Then I began to think about how so many Christians either do not understand, or they do not believe much of the truth of this freedom, and began to wonder why. Why is it so hard to see, understand and simply believe and live out the truths of Christ which God reveals powerfully to and in us?

The answer came to me in a revelational picture of a pinball machine. You pull back the spring-loaded knob and let it go, sending a steel ball out of the chute to the top of the machine, and gravity brings it down toward the exit chute. Ahhhh! Revelation!

But standing in the way of that ball's free and unhindered descent are obstacles, called bumpers, all over the place, most of which have their own spring-loaded mechanisms which, when struck by the ball, send it flying off in random directions. That ball is not free to go where it wants to go, the exit chute. In fact, even as it gets close to that exit chute, there is a very deliberate mechanism in place meant to keep it out ... the flippers!

So it is with well meaning Christians. They read the Word of God, and they desire to believe it and live it and see its truth manifested in their life. But when they try, so many obstacles to the truth's free expression seem to jump out and block their way. And I'm not just talking about carnally lustful type sins. There are trickier kinds.

For example, maybe a believer reads the following in their Bible.

Stand fast therefore in the liberty with which Christ has made us free, and be no longer entangled again with the yoke of bondage. (Galatians 5:1)

Maybe they read it themselves in their own personal Bible study, or with others in a group study, or maybe they hear it read and preached at Church on Sunday. Okay, the words themselves have entered their head, but has the truth of the words entered their heart? Not necessarily.

There are bumpers and flippers in every Church ... practices, or ways of seeing things, of living out what is supposed to be the life of God, but which in truth hamper the hungry soul from growing into Christ. The preacher reads, "You are free in Christ." But do you think he is going to add, "That means you are free not to come to Church on Sunday?" I don't think so.

He's going to say something, interpret this verse, in a way which keeps his flock close to their Church home, closely bound to their pastor and his congregation. Perhaps he's going to say that freedom means we can do our Christian tasks, lead our Christian lives, with joy in our heart, with love for others ... and others will see that joy and love and want what we have; want to come to church with you. But Galatians 5:1 doesn't talk about love or joy, or about bringing others to church ... it talks about freedom!

But as then he who was born after the flesh persecuted him who was born after the Spirit, even so it is now. (Galatians 4:29)

The Christian (pastor, pope, young believer - anyone) who is walking by his flesh will not be an encouragement to the one who desires to be led by the Spirit of God. That bondage to flesh only desires more of the same … bondage to flesh. It can only be by a strict, disciplined desire to follow the Spirit's working all the way to the end, no matter how it looks to others, that a person gets to see what freedom in Christ is really all about.

> *Therefore, brethren, we are debtors, not to the flesh, to live after the flesh. (Romans 8:12)*

Otherwise, a Christian could read the following verse.

> *For brethren, you have been called unto liberty; only use not liberty for an occasion to the flesh, but by love serve one another. (Galatians 5:13)*

And because of the pinball bumpers and flippers which confront his desire to see the truth of this verse manifest in his life, he could think that serving one another means telling another Christian who doesn't share the same Christian doctrine as he does that they are going to hell if they don't change their belief. Maybe he'll harshly and condemningly reprove someone because they used a four letter word, telling them to "watch their witness." Maybe he'll demand from one of his friends that if they really loved God, they wouldn't ever miss Church on Sunday, like they have been doing lately.

Why would a Christian behave in such a way toward others? This is not the truth of God's Word being manifested in and through their lives. Rather, it is the example they've been given at their church, or among their Christian friends, or by their pastor; or perhaps it is them being tricked by the devil directly. These erroneous examples are obstacles to true spiritual growth.

> *You hypocrites, well did Isaiah prophesy of you, saying, This*

people draws near unto me with their mouth, and honors me with their lips; but their heart is far from me. And in vain they do worship me, teaching for doctrines the commandments of men. (Matthew 15:7, 8)

All of these erroneous ways of seeing and interpreting and manifesting the truths of the Word of God are like the bumpers in a pinball game. They don't allow the truth of God's Word, of Christ, to find its (super)natural way into living itself out in a person's life. Rather they are obstacles in the path of truth, sending one who is seeking the spirit of freedom's true manifestation flying off in directions never intended. They are bumpers and flippers of erroneous understanding and perspective and behavior which have been implemented and established by the enemy of God, intended solely to keep people away from the glorious fruit of the spirit's true manifestation.

How can you believe, who receive honor (doxa - glory) one of another, and seek not the honor (glory) that comes from the only God? (John 5:44)

If your pursuit of truth and its manifestation needs to be filtered through the approval of others, no matter who they are (friend, father, pastor, pope), then you will never be free to follow Christ. Rather, you will be stuck in a religious rut of understanding, interpretation and application which limits your access to God and the true and free expression of that relationship.

The idea of "accountability" to another Christian is a spiritual bumper. It is nothing more than standing approved before man! Abide by it and be spiritually stunted, or sent off in unfruitful directions by good, well-meaning (fleshly) intentions.

The idea of needing to obey your church's head pastor in all things is a spiritual flipper. It is standing approved before man! Need this flipper to make your spiritual decisions, or even to approve the working of Christ within you, and you'll live a spiritually stunted existence.

The idea of conforming your behavior to fit in with the way everyone else at your church does things is a pinball machine of impediments, obstacles, bumpers and flippers meant only to keep you from the glorious freedom of experiencing Christ as your true and vital spiritual head.

The truth is I have no idea what the freedom that you have in Christ is going to look like or where it's going to take you, as you grow and develop in your spiritual relationship with the Father. I can't even imagine how that freedom is going to play itself out in my own life, much less yours. But I do know that it will have the same character and nature as Christ. Your freedom … my freedom … Christ's freedom … all have the indelible character and nature of God's tender love.

Time to get rid of the preconceived notions of what a life in Christ should look like. Time to stand against the religious bumpers and flippers which have kept our lives from Christ's glorious freedom for so long. Time to see these things for what they really are - obstacles to spiritual growth and manifestation.

Every day can be an exciting experience of journey and discovery in the life of God. Seek Christ and allow his spirit within you to find uniquely personal expression in the world in which you live. Don't be afraid of the disapproval of others; in fact, it's pretty well guaranteed by God you'll face disapproval as long as you allow the spirit of Christ to lead your life.

If the world hate you, you know that it hated me before it hated you. If you were of the world, the world would love its own; but because you are not of the world, but I have chosen you out of the world, therefore the world hates you. (John 15:18, 19)

They shall put you out of the synagogues (churches)*; yea, the time comes that whosoever kills you will think the he does God service. And these things will they do unto you, because they have not known the Father, nor me. (John 16:2, 3)*

Rather than seeking or desiring the approval of man, realize you and Christ are going to live a fantastically unique, powerful, dynamic life. It is only in the discovery and experience of the spirit of Christ that we are birthed, completed, fulfilled and caused to grow and flourish in a way the world has never before seen. Enjoy the journey!

Therefore let no man glory in men. For all things are yours; Whether Paul, or Apollos, or Cephas (Peter) *or the world, or life, or death, or things present, or things to come; all are yours; And you are Christ's; and Christ is God's. (I Corinthians 3:21-23)*

RULED BY FLESHLY RESPONSIBILITY

Romans 8:12 continues the truth that the mind of the flesh is in a state of conflict or war with God, because it cannot receive the things of the spirit of Christ, which are freely given as a gift by God.

> *Therefore, brethren, we are debtors, not to the flesh, to live after the flesh. For if you live after the flesh, you shall die; but if you through the spirit do mortify the deeds of the body, you shall life. For as many as are led by the spirit of God, they are the sons of God. (Romans 8:12)*

Most people live indebted to the flesh. To job, family, friends, church, their emotions, health, etc. Their lives are ruled by fleshly and psychological responsibility. Many embrace this duty, others try to avoid it; but in any case, this sense of responsibility rules their lives. Whether embracing it or running from it, this sense of obligation in and to our fleshly life is a powerful, all-encompassing, unrelenting force which must be dealt with continually.

From the time we wake up in the morning (sometimes it even keeps us up at nights) until we close our eyes and welcome sleep at night, the needs, obligations, duties, and responsibilities we have in our fleshly lives and minds and feelings are demanding our attention and fealty. They want to rule our minds and hearts, and they indicate to us that they will not go quietly away until they have been met, served, accomplished, maintained and/or finished; but they seem to never finish and they never willingly depart.

Most Christians think that being responsible is God's will, so they serve this fleshly indebtedness with a high moral attitude, as if them serving their flesh is a Godly response to their being saved by grace. But this is erroneous! God did not send His son to save us so that we could become extremely responsible in the flesh! The world says, "The reward for work well done is more work." God says otherwise. He says, "The reward for work well done is rest."

And on the seventh day God ended His work which He had made; and He rested on the seventh day from all His work which He had made. And God blessed the seventh day, and sanctified it; because that in it He had rested from all His work which God created and made. (Genesis 2:2)

The awareness of the mind which lives so indebted to the flesh is that only death will free it from this responsibility. And here is where the death of Jesus Christ has done its perfect work; that dying, Jesus has freed us from the powerful need to walk in any indebtedness to the flesh ... at all! By his death he freed me from any fleshly indebtedness, because his death served as my death, as regards any fleshly debt.

For he that is dead is freed from sin (and its demands). *(Romans 6:7)*

Well thank you very much! I am now freed from any indebtedness to my flesh, but I am dead, so I don't even know I'm free, much less am able to enjoy my freedom. In death what will you do? Nothing. (Contrary to what many believe, death is not a welcome friend, but an enemy which Jesus Christ overcame). But because he died for me, I can enjoy being debt free while still alive!

> *Now since we be dead with Christ, we believe that we shall also* (now) *live with him; (Romans 6:8)*

I took a look in my trusty E.W. Bullinger's *A Critical Lexicon and Concordance to the English and Greek New Testament* for the word "responsibility" or "responsible" and I could see that neither one of those words is used a single time in the New Testament! Then I took my *Young's Analytical Concordance to the Bible* and found the same to be true for the Old Testament. Neither "responsible" nor "responsibility" are ever found in the King James Version of the Bible ... anywhere!

What about responsibility to my family? What about responsibility to my job, my friends, my self? What about responsibility to my church, my religion, my moral obligations?

> *Let us hear the conclusion of the whole matter; Fear God, and keep His commandments; for this is the whole duty of man. (Ecclesiastes 12:13)*

Until you have died to self, to your need to satisfy your flesh's moral demands, you cannot serve God. Until you are seated in Christ at the right hand of his Father, God, you will be talked out of serving Him. Until your indebtedness to Christ overrules your indebtedness to the flesh, you will be ruled by your flesh.

> *Since you are then risen with Christ, seek those things which are above, where Christ is seated at the right hand of God. Set your affection on things above, not on things which are on the earth; For you are dead, and your life is hid with Christ in God. (Colossians 3:1-4)*

When you believed unto Jesus Christ, you became a new man,

a man alive! That righteousness of God which became yours the moment you first believed unto Jesus was the gift of God's life born within you, at which time the old you died. You cannot live your old life and successfully live your new life in Christ. If you were dead and in the ground you would do nothing to satisfy your fleshly responsibilities. In Christ your fleshly indebtedness has disappeared, because your old self with its obligations has died.

I have experienced many Christians unable to pursue the things of God because they are so frazzled from keeping all their responsibilities of this earthly life. Their responsibilities to wife and children, to earning money to pay the bills, to parents, to their own entertainment, to their own "down time." Yet they seem to have no time for seeking Christ. These are wonderful believers with sweet, compassionate hearts, having their spiritual life choked out of them by their fleshly responsibilities.

> *Let us therefore fear, lest, a promise being left us of entering into His rest, any of you should seem to come short of it. For unto us was the gospel preached, as well as unto them; but the word preached did not profit them, not being mixed with faith in them that heard. (Hebrews 4:1, 2)*

They didn't believe God had done it all, but rather carried on in their unbelief in their indebtedness to fleshly responsibility. They said, "God supplies my needs" and then thought it was their responsibility to worry about where the money would come from to pay the bills.

> *For we who have believed do enter into rest, as He said, "As I have sworn in my wrath that they shall not enter into my rest;" though indeed the works were finished from the foundation of the world. (Hebrews 4:3)*

Israel was promised "the promised land." It was sitting there waiting for them. Theirs for the taking. God told them it was theirs for the taking, but the people chose to believe 10 out of the 12 "spies" who were sent to search out the land, who reported that the inhabitants of the promised land were too great to conquer, that they (Israel) would not be able to take the land from them. And so they "wandered" in wilderness for 40 years in their unbelief until those who did not believe had died. Even though God had given Israel the promised land 40 years earlier, (to God it was a done deal) the people chose not to believe it, staying indebted to their fleshly abilities and responsibilities and limitations.

> *There remains therefore a rest to the people of God. For he that is entered into His rest, he also has ceased from his own works, as God did from His. Let us labor therefore to enter into that rest, lest any man fall after the same example of unbelief. (Hebrews 4:10, 11)*

It is much easier to believe that Jesus died for your sins when you feel guilty about them, than to accept the rest of God which is rightfully yours in Christ! It is so much easier to continue to try to alleviate the pressure of your earthly responsibility than it is to rest in the peace and righteous holiness which is freely given you by Christ Jesus. It is much easier to continue on in your fleshly indebtedness than it is to simply believe that Christ is enough. God says, "Okay, you've come to Christ. I've got it from here." And we say, "Thanks but no thanks, I've got responsibilities to keep!" And thus we reject the offering of God, which is Christ Jesus the Lord.

You will surely say to me, "But I've got to feed my family. But I've given my word. But I've got duties to maintain." And I will answer, "You died in Christ. Christ is your whole life! Seek Christ!"

> *I was crucified with Christ, nevertheless I live, yet not I, but Christ lives in me, and the life which I now live in the flesh I live by the faith of the son of God, who loved me and gave*

himself for me. (Galatians 2:20)

I can live my life in Christ, having his thoughts my thoughts, his heart my heart, his priorities my priorities and still work, feed my family, train my children, take care of myself. But my life in him is number 1; greater than my marriage, my health, my children; my profession. And when he speaks, I listen, and in him I have only one responsibility:

Owe no man anything, but to love one another; (Romans 13:8a)

The mind of earthly responsibility cannot love another with God's love, for that mind does not have God's love to give. It is too busy paying its never-ending debt to the flesh, so that it can not freely accept and walk in the giftings and fruitfulness of the spirit of Christ. Boil your life down to this: Seek Christ and walk in his love – that is the core of your whole duty to God.

Wherefore I also, having heard of your faith in the Lord Jesus, and love unto all the saints, cease not to give thanks for you … (Ephesians 1:15, 16a)

DEAD WORKS AND THE SPIRITUAL RAIN DANCE

I Kings 17 & 18 contain a fantastic record of a time of drought and Israel's deliverance from that drought by the hand of Elijah, the prophet of the true God. Before deliverance came, there was a contest between Elijah and the prophets of Ba-al (a fertility god, also known as a storm god, one of the main gods of that region's pagans) as to who's god could bring down fire from heaven.

> *And Elijah said unto the prophets of Ba-al, Choose you one bullock for yourselves, and dress it first; for you are many* (there were 450 of them!), *and call on the name of your gods, but put no fire under. And they took the bullock which was given them, and they dressed it, and called on the name of Ba-al from morning even until noon, saying, O Ba-al, hear us. But there was no voice, nor any that answered. And they leaped upon the altar which was made. And it came to pass at noon, that Elijah mocked them, and said, Cry aloud; for he is a god; either he is talking, or he is pursuing, or he is in a journey, or perhaps he is sleeping, and must be awakened. And they cried aloud, and cut themselves after their manner with knives and lancets, till the blood gushed out upon them. And it came to pass, when midday*

was past, and they prophesied until the time of the offering of the evening sacrifice, that there was neither voice nor any to answer, nor any that regarded. (I Kings 18:25-29)

Why is it so hard to please God?! What more does He want anyway? How come I never seem to do enough!?! I guess I just have to do more!

For if the blood of bulls and of goats and the ashes of a heifer sprinkling the unclean sanctifies to the purifying of the flesh; How much more shall the blood of Christ, who by means of the eternal Spirit offered himself without spot to God, purge your conscience from dead works to serve the living God? (Hebrews 9:13, 14)

Chapters 7-10 in Hebrews, and really the whole book of Hebrews, juxtaposes the Old Testament of the law of Moses with the New Testament of the sacrifice and ministry today of Jesus Christ. Though this rather long letter was written for the benefit of Jewish believers, who had a very difficult time escaping the bondage of living under the law of Moses (including the 10 Commandments), the Christian Church of today can very much benefit from it, being very much in the same predicament.

The word "purge" in the above verse means a winnowing, cleansing or pruning. Your conscience will not change overnight from a need to do works in order to please God, to one of freely and thankfully receiving the blessings of God by means of the completed work of Jesus Christ. Rather it is only through a faithfully applied effort of will toward Christ that we come more and more into a place of having no need to do works for God's love. Like is written in Hebrews 4:11a: "Let us labor therefore to come into that rest...."

And for this reason he is the mediator of the New Testament, that by means of death, for the redemption of the transgressions that were under the first testament (the Old Testament)*, they*

who were called might receive the promise of eternal inheritance.
(Hebrews 9:15)

The word "Testament" should really be rendered "Covenant." It's a contractual agreement between two parties. The old testament, or covenant, God had with His people (Israel) was given by Moses, and the agreement was very strongly worded. God said, over and over again, "If you do this, I will do this," and "If you do not do this, I will not do this - or I will do this (terrible thing)." In addition, the demands of this old agreement never ceased until death. There was no resting on what you did or didn't do yesterday, the agreement had to continually be kept.

So the works that God demanded from His people under this old agreement were in order to earn His blessing, or to avoid deserving His punishment. Unfortunately, the majority of the Christian Church of today operates under this same old agreement with God. You want God's blessing? Then you'd better toe the line, obey the rules. You'd better put out your very best efforts or don't expect anything good from God. ("You do your best and God will do the rest"). In fact, if you blow it, don't be surprised when the punishment of God comes raining down upon your head.

Jesus Christ established a new agreement, a new contract, with God. Unlike the old, it was a one-and-done deal that ushered in this new covenant.

> *By the which will* (God's) *we are sanctified by means of the offering of the body of Jesus Christ once. But this man, after he had offered one sacrifice for sins forever, sat down on the right hand of God; For by one offering he has perfected forever those who are sanctified. (Hebrews 10:10, 12, 14)*

The teaching of today's Christian Church, when it even takes the time to make known the Word of God, seems for the most part to have a particular love for the Old Testament, the old agreement

God had with His people. The Church today teaches of doing works in order to please God, of making sure not to displease God lest we incur His wrath.

The Church today, for the most part, seems to delight in teaching, "Jesus gets you started, but you better then prove yourself worthy of what he did … or else!" This is so *not* the truth of today!

If you read the Old Testament and of the requirement of works in order to please God, you should be reading it in thankfulness that it no longer applies to you; for the perfect sacrifice of Jesus Christ has eliminated the need for any other person to ever do any other work in order to please God. That's right! No more works are required by God in order for Him to be able to pour out every blessing possible upon our heads, into our hearts, and flowing out of our lives and into the lives of others.

> *Blessed be the God and Father of our Lord Jesus Christ, Who has blessed us with every spiritual blessing in the heavenlies* (the spiritual realm) *in Christ. (Ephesians 1:3)*

The only good works God wants from us today, under His new agreement with His people, are those which flow out of the working of the spirit of Christ within us, where that spirit both initiates and empowers that work.

> *For it is God who works in you both to will and to do of His good pleasure. (Philippians 2:13)*

If you are not in the spirit of God (another way of saying "in Christ") then you cannot please God, no matter how many "good" works you do. All your thinking and reasoning and deciding and planning and doing are "dead works" if they are not inspired by and flow out of the spirit of Christ.

I hope this does not sound like an impossible task to you, but rather an exciting challenge. To explore life in Christ as we learn to be loved by the living God, this is our primary and only "job." Outside the spirit of Christ are found only dead works. Outside God's completed work in and of Christ is found only a spiritual rain-dance; going through a lot of thoughts and emotions and works and agonizings of the mind and heart in our endeavor to earn our right standing with God, but that do absolutely nothing to please God or to earn His blessing in our lives.

So the next time the thought comes into your heart that maybe God isn't working in your life because you haven't done enough good works, claim the finished work of Jesus Christ as all that is needed to receive the blessings of God. The next time you get "inspired" to do a bunch of good deeds so that God will love you more, just give up and lay down at the feet of the living Christ. If Christ is not all you need, then he didn't do enough, then God lied and we're still living under the old agreement with Him, and the Old Testament still applies.

Following are some of the thoughts/condemnations which flow out of the thinking of dead works and the need for a spiritual rain-dance in order to please God:

> I gotta go to Church this Sunday or something bad will happen, because God won't like me.

> I was angry with my friend, so I'd better do something to make it better so I'll still be in God's good graces.

> I know, I'll read the whole Bible, then I'll really be able to serve God.

> Maybe if I talk to 10 people a day about Jesus and God and the Bible, God will accept me.

> If I go on this missions trip, then I'll be liked by the Pastor and

I'll be spiritual.

I need to raise my hands while everyone's singing (like everyone else) in order to be spiritual.

God likes it when I sing really loud and sincerely in Church.

I'll get involved in every event planned by my Church....that'll earn me blessings from God.

I haven't said I'm sorry enough for all my sins, maybe that's why I don't feel closer to God.

People don't like me; they misunderstand me....I must be doing something wrong.

The one thing in common with all the above thoughts is that they all have nothing to do with Jesus Christ and his sacrifice and gift. Christ is all you need, now and forever. Seek him, explore him, study him, apply your head and heart to him, and walk in the new agreement of the righteous blessings of God, which are only found in Christ Jesus our Lord, for all your days.

And he (Elijah) *put the wood in order , and cut the bullock in pieces, and laid it on the wood, and said, Fill four barrels with water, and pour it on the burnt sacrifice, and on the wood. And he said, Do it the second time. And they did it the second time. And he said, Do it the third time. And they did it the third time. And the water ran round about the altar; and he filled the trench also with water. And it came to pass at the time of the offering of the evening sacrifice, that Elijah the prophet came near, and said, Lord God of Abraham, Isaac, and of Israel, let it be known this day that You are God in Israel, and that I am Your servant, and that I have done all these things at Your word. Hear me, O Lord, hear me, that this people may know that You are the Lord God, and that You have turned their heart back again. Then the fire of the Lord fell, and consumed the burnt sacrifice, and the wood, and the stones, and the dust, and licked up the water that was in the trench. And when all the people saw it, they fell on their faces: and they said, The Lord He is the God; the Lord, He is the God! (I Kings 18:33-39)*

The only way to get Godly results is to let God do it His way!

GLORY

The full and unhindered expression

HALF A GOSPEL

There are 2 halves to the true Gospel.

> *Then said Jesus unto them again, Verily, verily I say unto you, I am the door for the sheep. (John 10:7)*

This is the first half of the gospel. Jesus is the door. When you see a door, do you go to it, open it, and stand in the doorway? Is that the purpose for the door?

> *I am the door; by me if any man enter in, he shall be saved* (made whole)*, and shall go in and out, and find pasture. (John 10:9)*

There's the second half of the gospel. By means of the doorway, you'll be able to enter safely into enjoying all that God's creation has to offer. But many Christians get to that doorway, and they stop. And they look back, and continue to only stand in the doorway. They say, "I never depart from the cross." Never forget, the doorway is only the means to an end.

> *He that spared not His own son, but delivered him up for us all, (Romans 8:32a)*

This is the first half of the gospel. The crucifixion of Jesus Christ.

His payment for the sins of the world.

... how shall He not with him also freely give us all things? (Romans 8:32b)

There's the second half. Walking into the pasture of all that God has designed for us to do and have and enjoy. We don't want to simply be forgiven for our sins. In the freedom that forgiveness imparts to us, we want to sojourn forth into an exploration of the inheritance God has provided for His children.

For if, when we were enemies, we were reconciled to God by the death of His son, (1st half) (Romans 5:10a)

… much more, being reconciled, we shall be saved (made whole) *by his life. (2nd half) (Romans 5:10b)*

The death of Jesus Christ is our doorway into a relationship with God. By Jesus' death, we were reconciled (brought back into harmony) with God. Once in harmony, let's focus on making music!

For God so loved the world, that He gave His only begotten son; that whosoever believes unto him should not perish (1st half), but have everlasting life (2nd half). (John 3:16)

For if we have been planted together in the likeness of his death, (1st half) we shall be also in the likeness of his resurrection (2nd half): (Romans 6:5)

What good is metamorphosis if the butterfly doesn't fly? What good is building the house if it's never lived in? What good is buying the book if its never read? What good is working if you don't enjoy the fruit of your labor? What good is the death of Jesus Christ, if there is no life of glory?

Knowing that Christ being raised from the dead dies no more … (Romans 6:9a)

Okay, I'll stop with the "1st half" and "2nd half" parentheses. I'll let you see the 2 parts of the gospel yourselves. After reading this study, I'll expect that you won't be able to read of the death of Jesus Christ anymore, without anticipating reading in the same context of the ongoing benefits of his resurrection and glorification.

> *In whom we have redemption through his blood, the forgiveness of sins, according to the riches of His grace; Wherein He has abounded toward us in all wisdom and prudence* (common sense thinking)*; Having made known unto us the mystery of His will, according to His good pleasure which He has purposed in Himself; That in the administration of the fullness of times He might gather together in one all things in Christ, both which are in heaven, and which are on earth; even in him; In whom also we have obtained an inheritance, (Ephesians 1:7-11a)*

Both parts of the gospel are not always mentioned in the same verse, but both parts are always mentioned together.

> *And you, who were once alienated and enemies in your mind by wicked works, yet now has he reconciled In the body of his flesh through death, to present you holy and unblameable and unreprovable in His sight; (Colossians:1:21, 22)*

> *The mystery, which has been hid from ages and from generations, but now is made manifest to His saints; That their hearts might be comforted, being knit together in love, and unto all riches of the full assurance of understanding, to the acknowledgment of the mystery of God - Christ; In whom are hid all the treasures of wisdom and knowledge. (Colossians 1:27, 2:2, 3)*

You see, what good is forgiveness by God or reconciliation with God, if their is no ongoing benefit of that reconciliatory forgiveness?

I was estranged from my earthly father when I was a young man and out on my own. I had animosity toward him, not having forgiven him for divorcing my mother. But while living far from home, in Florida, I came to forgive my father and wrote to him announcing my forgiveness. Now yes, I felt good after writing that letter. But what benefit would there have been to that forgiveness if I had not sought after and obtained a healthy father/son relationship afterward? If, when I returned to live in Wisconsin, where my father lived, I did not develop and enjoy a good relationship with him?

Well, I did develop a lovingly healthy relationship with my father after our reconciliation. Because of that reconciliation, I was able to enjoy many warm-hearted and joyfully rewarding experiences with him before he died. I did not stop at forgiveness. I moved into a rich and rewarding relationship.

What kind of gospel do you claim, if you keep kneeling at the cross of Jesus Christ, but do not go on and explore his resurrected, glorified life within you? Standing in the doorway of the cross is not the intention of our loving heavenly Father. Rather, God intended His children to come into His warm embrace, where sin will never again be a problem between us; but rather where His glorious fullness can now be richly enjoyed and expressed by His beloved children ... *despite sin*! Where the inheritance He has intended for us can be experienced and felt every day from now and into eternity!

This is why I so enjoy the Pauline epistles. Paul was tasked by God to make known the riches of God's inheritance provided by the 2nd half of the Gospel; to reveal to the saints the ongoing work of the glorified Christ, whose life enlivens and glorifies us today.

The first half of the Gospel happened once, and the power of that completed act continues to change people in a moment of time. But the second half of the Gospel is an ongoing work, being performed by our living Lord and Savior, Jesus Christ, now and forever!

> *I am crucified with Christ; nevertheless I live; yet not I, but Christ lives in me; and the life which I now live in the flesh I live by the faith of the Son of God, who loved me, and gave himself for me. (Galatians 2:20)*

Do you see it? The death of Christ paid for our sin, once and for all. It's a one time deal. But the living we can now do in relationship with our heavenly Father; why, that's a deal that goes on and on for an eternity!

> *That in the ages to come He might exhibit the exceeding* (hyperbolic) *riches of His grace in kindness toward us in Christ Jesus. (Ephesians 2:7)*

HOW TO WALK WORTHY
OF GOD

As you know how we exhorted and comforted and charged every one of you, as a father does his children, That you would walk worthy of God, Who has called you unto His kingdom and glory. (I Thessalonians 2:11, 12)

The word "worthy" is the Greek word *axios*, and is best understood by understanding it's root word, ago, which means "to bring." This root word is used 71x in the New Testament, and is translated "to bring" or "to lead."

This root word ago is first used in:

(Jesus is speaking to his newly appointed apostles) *But beware of men; for they will deliver you up to the councils, and they will scourge* (whip) *you in their synagogues; And you shall be brought (ago) before governors and kings for my sake, for a testimony against them and the Gentiles. (Matthew 10:17, 18)*

It will not be the apostles' own idea to go before governors and kings to receive judgment, and possibly condemnation and punishment, from the civil authorities; rather, they would be brought. And rather than fight against this "bringing", they were to allow it to happen.

> (Jesus) *Saying unto them, Go into the village over against you, and immediately you shall find an ass tied, and a cold with her; loose them and bring (ago) them unto me. (Matthew 21:2)*

Those animals did not decide on their own to walk to Jesus, they were led. Rather than question, argue, resist or rebel, they allowed themselves to be brought by others to Jesus.

> *And Jesus being full of the Holy Spirit returned from Jordan* (where he was baptized by John), *and was led (ago) by the Spirit into the wilderness. (Luke 4:1)*

This leading was from within, for Jesus was "led" or brought by the holy spirit with which he was filled. It therefore took place within his heart and mind, and then played itself out in his actions. He did not fight against it, but rather allowed himself to be brought by the Spirit into the wilderness, and then to be tempted by the devil for 40 days.

And so we start to get a flavor of what "worthy" means. When you allow yourself to be brought by an influence to the place which that influence wants to bring you, you are worthy of that influence.

If I'm a college basketball player, and I allow myself to be brought to the level of mature play the coach wants to bring me, I am then worthy of his coaching. When an apple allows itself to be grown from an apple tree and brought to the point of maturity where it can then reproduce another apple tree, or which tastes delicious when eaten, it is a worthy apple. When a doctor is able to save someone's life, he is worthy of the education which brought him to that place.

Now back to I Thessalonians 2:12. We walk "worthy of God" by allowing God to bring us (by heeding His calling of us - which takes place in the heart) into His kingdom and glory. This worthiness comes as we allow God to do what He's always wanted to do in us and for us.

"Into His kingdom and glory" is another way of saying "Into His kingdom, which is His glory." Both these words, "kingdom" and "glory" are descriptions of the same thing. "Kingdom" emphasizes that this is where His will dominates all others' will, and "glory" emphasizes that it is Him fully expressing Himself! God has called us into an existence where His will, that our lives are full, complete and unhindered expressions of God Himself, is a continuous reality!

How can we hope to walk worthy of God? Impossible by our own efforts! Possible only by allowing ourselves to be led by the call of the spirit of Christ to the place in our minds and hearts that God's desire to express Himself in and through us rules the day!

> *I therefore the prisoner of the Lord, beseech you that you walk worthy of the vocation with which you are called. (Ephesians 4:1)*

A more accurate translation of the latter part of this verse would be, "...that you walk worthy of the calling (laleo) with which you were called out (eklaleo)." This last "called out" is the verb form of the word which is translated "church" throughout the New Testament (ekklesia). The church of God are those who have responded at one time to God's calling in their lives, making them the "called out" (church) of God.

In this verse is the key to how to walk worthy of God. Simply continue to respond to the calling of His holy spirit within, which you originally responded to. And then God describes for us how His calling will continue to work within us.

With all lowliness (humility) *and meekness, with longsuffering, forbearing one another in love; Endeavoring to keep the unity of the spirit in the bond of peace. (Ephesians 4:2)*

"With all" means every bit you can find.

"Humility" is the conscious affirmation of our inferiority to and need for God; His wisdom, His power, His life and love. His ways are so far beyond our own.

"Meekness" is the open-heartedness we have as one that has not "arrived." It is the spiritual ability to grasp life from another's point of view.

"Longsuffering" is the loving allowance of others' weakness and inability.

"Forbearing" is the generous carrying of another's load.

"Unity" = oneness

"Bond" = glue

In the welcoming safety of God's loving presence in our lives, we are fully connected with one another.

Make conscious effort to heed God's call in your heart and life. Thus will God make you worthy of Himself. Allow God to continue to do what He first did when you first believed unto Jesus Christ. That is how you walk worthy of God. Simply desire what He desires; which is to bring you to the place in Christ where His will is supreme, where His nature is able to be fully expressed in all its glory.

And he that takes not his cross, and follows after me, is not worthy of me. He that finds his life shall lose it; and he that loses his life for my sake shall find it. (Matthew 10:38, 39)

We follow after Jesus by allowing ourselves to be led by the spirit of Christ, not by trying to bend the world to our will. In Christ is God's calling perfected. In Christ is God's will brought into reality. In Christ God brings us to the place of being worthy of Him.

> *You are worthy, O Lord and our God, to receive glory and honor and power (dunamis); for You have created all things, and for Your pleasurable will they are, and were created. (Revelation 4:11)*

This "walk" is a walk of the mind and heart. It happens in the innermost part of our being, in our most intimate thinking and reasoning, deciding and planning. And to that innermost part of who we are, God's call to us will forever be, "Come, give yourself over to being led by My spirit, and walk worthy of Me!"

WHAT IS GLORY

Many words have a religious connotation. When you hear a phrase like "the glory of God", all you're likely to think is "God/religion/holy/Bible/love/Jesus/prayer/heaven/hell/try not to sin." I've discovered through the years of my Biblical studies and research that I do not like defining the words of the Bible using a religious context. Because then, my understanding of that word will only have meaning in my experience of religion; that is, at church or in some other religious gathering.

Rather, I want God to be a part of every facet of my life. And so, understanding the words of the Word of God in light of everyday usage is very important. This is why Jesus taught using parables, in which everyday situations were presented as representing the truths of the kingdom of God.

Glory is from the Greek word *doxa*.

It means (and this is the revelational understanding I've come up with - I encourage you to come up with your own). the full and unhindered expression of the best of someone or something, which elicits admiration in the observer.

Example: the winner of the 100 meter dash at the Olympics. He might be the fastest in the world, but his glory is when he wins the race and expresses or manifests that speed for all to see and admire. His glory is not expressed when he's riding the bus, or working at a convenience store (even though he's still the fastest man in the world).

The first use of *doxa* in the New Testament:

> *Again, the devil takes him up into an exceeding high mountain, and shows him all the kingdoms of the world, and the glory (doxa) of them. (Matt 4:8)*

Consider the glory of the United States. Some examples are: the freedom its citizens have to express ideas, to move about freely, to benefit from their own industriousness. The prosperity and inventiveness and productivity they display. The natural beauty of its mountains, coasts, deserts, forests, etc. These things are the glory of the United States.

> *And suddenly there was with the angel a multitude of the heavenly host praising God, and saying, Glory (doxa) to God in the highest, and on earth peace, good will toward men. (Luke 2:13, 14)*

To "give glory to God" only happens when, or after, God's glory is manifested (in this instance the birth of His son). It means to recognize and credit that glory to the one glorified (God's best was fully expressed, or manifested). When someone says, "I give God all the glory", that person is really saying "I give God all the credit," or "I recognize God's expression of Himself and publicly acknowledge it."

> *But when you are invited, go and sit down in the lowest room; that when he that invited you comes, he may say unto you, Friend, go up higher; then shall you have worship (doxa - glory)*

in the presence of them that sit at meat with you. (Luke 14:10)

Many of you recognize this instruction by Jesus concerning those who chose to sit in the places of greatest distinction. The custom in the east during a feast or party was that when everyone sat down to eat, the greatest, or most important people at the party sat closest to the host, the one throwing the party. When one was asked to come and sit closer, the best was conferred upon that person, and was observed with admiration in all those who sat around. In this instance of glory, the best came from (was conferred by) another.

And the Word was made flesh, and dwelt among us, (and we beheld his glory (doxa), the glory (doxa) as of the only begotten of the Father), full of grace and truth. (John 1:14)

For the Son of man shall come in the glory (doxa) of his Father with his angels; and then he shall reward every man according to his works. (Matt 16:27)

The glory of Jesus Christ while he was on this earth was the glory of his Father. Jesus' glory was conferred by his Father. (Regarding rewarding each man according to his works, remember this was spoken to Jews who were under the law).

I receive not honor (doxa - glory) from men. But I know you, that you have not the love of God in you. I am come in my Father's name, and you receive me not; if another shall come in his own name, him you will receive. How can you believe, who receive honor (doxa) one of another, and seek not the honor (doxa) that comes from God only. (John 5:41-44)

Jesus did not get promoted, was never given the best, by man. He came to serve and not to be served. We grow in our believing of God (in our relationship with Him) as we seek that full expression of ourselves which only God can make happen. To the degree that we seek what man has to offer us to add to our lives, we stagnate in our growth of believing God.

Jesus answered, I have not a devil; but I honor my Father, and you do dishonor me. And I seek not my own glory (doxa); there is one that seeks and judges. (John 8:49, 50)

> *Because that, when they knew God, they glorified* (verb form of *doxa*) *him not as God, neither were thankful; but became vain in their imaginations* (logical reasonings)*, and their foolish heart was darkened. Professing themselves to be wise, they became fools. And changed the glory (doxa) of the incorruptible God into an image made like to corruptible man, and to birds, and four-footed beasts, and creeping things. (Romans 1:21-23)*

> *Howbeit we speak wisdom among them that are perfect* (mature)*; yet not the wisdom of this world, nor of the princes of this world, that come to nought; But we speak the wisdom of God in a mystery, even the hidden wisdom, which God ordained* (prepared) *before the world unto our glory (doxa); Which none of the princes of this world knew; for had they known it, they would not have crucified the Lord of glory (doxa). (I Corinthians 2:6-8)*

The truth is that our full expression, the full and unhindered expression of our greatness, occurs in the context of this mystery. Kind of makes you want to know the mystery, doesn't it? In (very) short, the mystery is how Christ works individually and powerfully in each member of his body, causing all things (of him) to work together for good. It is how each and every working of Christ benefits not only the individual, but how it benefits every other member of the body of Christ also, by means of the spiritual bonds that hold us together as one body.

Until the day of Pentecost, when the glory of this mystery began to be manifested in the world by the spirit now born within man, it was held as a closely guarded secret in the deepest heart of God. In its understanding and experience lies the fullness of our glory. We cannot be complete and fulfilled without it.

I encourage you to pick up your Bibles and read Ephesians 1. *Doxa* is used several times and is translated "glory" every time. God's full expression in us is our glory, and it is important to gain an understanding that God's full expression in and through us is His intended purpose for us for all eternity. Over time, as we experience His glory, we become His glory, the glory of Christ within.

> *According as His divine power* (*dunamis* - ability) *has given unto us all things that pertain unto life and godliness, through the knowledge* (*epignosis* – intimate experiential knowing) *of Him who has called us to glory and virtue* (excellence)*: Whereby are given unto us exceeding great and precious promises; that by these you might be partakers* (share fully) *of the divine nature, … (II Peter 1:3, 4a)*

> *Unto which* (salvation - a whole life) *He called you by our gospel to the obtaining of the glory of our Lord Jesus Christ. (II Thessalonians 2:14)*

LOVE OF THE UNKNOWN

The world has raised us to fear the unknown, but God designed His children to be explorers and adventurers. Our spiritual Father has instilled in His children an exciting love and anticipation for what lies just around that next corner. He has equipped us, not only to be able to handle whatever comes our way, but to grow and blossom in ever-expanding fruitfulness by means of every challenging experience.

> *And God is able to make all grace abound toward you; that you, always having all sufficiency in all things, may abound to every good work: (II Corinthians 9:8)*

God is able! And the character of His ability lives in each one of us, His children.

> *According as His divine power (dunamis - ability) has given unto us all things that pertain unto life and godliness, through the knowledge (epignosis) of Him who has called us to glory and virtue (excellence): Whereby are given unto us exceeding great and precious promises; that by these you might be partakers (share fully) of the divine nature, ... (II Peter 1:3, 4a)*

When man ate of the tree of the knowledge of good and evil, he came into the bondage of the vanity of his own mind, and he began living by the limitations of his own ability to know and understand. Thus, he lives in darkness, fear and susceptibility to Satan's offerings of that which he does not know or understand. But this is not how he was created by God.

> *And God said, Let us make man in our image, after our likeness … (Genesis 1:26a)*

There are two different words used here. "Image" and "likeness." They are not the same words. "Image" means an imprint, like that made with a metal or wooden stamp, and indicates that the very nature of man was to be like God's. "Likeness" means a pattern, indicating that man's abilities were to be God's abilities, to the end that man was to live like God lives, to know like He knows, to experience like He experiences.

Do you think that God lives in fear of what lies ahead? I don't. I think he meets every moment with loving boldness and excited anticipation. And man is a very important part of that lifestyle! We have been destined to live in and by the glory of God.

> *Unto which* (salvation - a whole life) *He called you by our gospel to the obtaining of the glory of our Lord Jesus Christ. (II Thessalonians 2:14)*

And what is the glory of our Lord Jesus Christ?

> *And what is the exceeding greatness of His power* (the hyperbolic *megathos* of His ability) *toward us who believe according to the working of His mighty power* (the strength of His overcoming ability) *Which He worked in Christ when He raised him from the dead and set him at His own right hand in the heavenlies, Far above all principality, and power, and might, and dominion, and every name that is named, not*

only in this age, but also in that which is to come; and has put all under his feet, and gave him to be the head over all for the church, Which is his body, the fullness of him who fulfills all in all. (Ephesians 1:19-23)

We, the church, are the fullness of him (Christ) who fulfills all in all. The glory of our Lord Jesus Christ is that he brings the design and purpose of God into reality in every person and in every situation; in every instance in every event. And we, the body of people in whom the spirit of Christ dwells, are the means by which this is carried out. Thus, the glory of the Lord Jesus Christ is the glory of us all, in whom the spirit of God is born.

Our lives have thus been promised the perfection of God's creative glory, but exactly how that creative glory will be expressed, how it will be played out, in each individual's life ... that remains to be seen and experienced.

For the earnest expectation of the creation waits for the manifestation of the sons of God. For the creation was made subject to vanity (in the garden), *(not willingly, but by reason of him* (the devil) *who has subjected the same) in hope. Because the creation itself also shall be delivered from the bondage of corruption into the glorious liberty of the children of God. (Romans 8:19-21)*

When man fell, he was kicked out of the garden, so that he would not eat of the tree of life, so that he would not stay fallen. Even man's vain mind desires and expects to be delivered from the crippling bondage such vanity imposes upon us. It is this hope, imparted by God Himself, which gives man the ability to love the unknown.

From the moment a house is built, it is in the bondage of corruption. With no outside help, a house will spring a leak here, a storm will cause a tree limb to break a window there, more and more the house will fall apart. It is in the bondage of corruption (as any homeowner will tell you!).

In contrast, the glorious liberty of the children of God is like a forest of trees. The trees will grow. Individual trees might burn, might be knocked down by winds, but the forest will grow, expand, thrive. This is the destiny of children of God. This is our hope!

> *For we know that the whole creation groans and travails in pain together until now. And not only it, but ourselves also, who have the firstfruits of the spirit, even we ourselves groan within ourselves, waiting for the adoption, the redemption of our body. For we are saved in hope: (Romans 8:22-24a)*

This is our calling, this is our hope, this is why we love the unknown. Life will never get boring, never become old and stale, as long as we are reaching with the wonder of exploration and discovery for that which lies ahead.

> *We give thanks to God and the Father of our Lord Jesus Christ, praying always for you, For the hope which is laid up for you in heaven* (the spiritual realm)*, of which you heard before in the word of the truth of the gospel; Which is come unto you, as in all the world, and brings forth fruit, as also in you, since the day you heard and knew (gnosko'd) the grace of God in truth. (Colossians 1:3, 5, 6)*

Well, there's the lifestyle of those born of the nature of God. We look forward to each new challenge, each new situation, every unexplored area of life and experience. With the ability of Christ (who is the image and glory of God) within, we are bound to live out (fulfill) all the good will and destiny of God. That we will succeed is a given, but exactly how that will "play itself out" remains to be seen. Let us enter into each day, situation, and relationship with loving anticipation of seeing the hand of God show itself in ways never before seen or experienced, as we reach out for the glory of God which has been promised us in Christ Jesus our Lord.

> *Brethren, I reckon (logizomai) not myself to have completely arrived at what I was destined for, but this one thing I do, forgetting those things which are behind, and reaching forth unto those things which are before, I press toward the mark for the prize of the high calling of God in Christ Jesus. (Philippians 3:13)*

I love what lies ahead, which I have yet to see, to understand, to be able to live out fully, to see manifested in and through my life. But I know as good as it's been, it's going to be that much better, and that much better, and that much better ....

What others say about "Give Me Christ - Revelations of the Glorified Christ, by Steve Hartlaub

Give Me Christ is a stunning work. Steve Hartlaub encapsulates vague/gray areas and difficult single issues of the Bible into concise chapters, which can be read in only minutes. His work gives understanding and power to fundamental scriptures. He has captured the simplicity of Christianity. It has always been amazing that Christ would say his "yoke is easy," yet when laws and errors are thrown back into doctrine, it gets complex and full of controversy—leaving condemnation, doubts, and questions. This book confirms the power of "Christ in us" with clear thinking and illuminates the Father's desire to converse with us while reading His Word. As you start realizing who you are, you will absolutely treasure who God has made you to be and what God has placed within you.

Sincerity (according to google) is the quality of being free from pretense, deceit, or hypocrisy. I do not think that this book is perfect....I do, however, find it to be a sincere, concise expression of the spirit of Christ within to which I have found NO comparison. If you desire freedom in the truest sense (starting from the faintest inkling of a neural-synapse in your deepest subconscious, and resonating out into every single facet of your very real and readily perceivable daily life) I sincerely hope that you take the time to delve into the truths contained within these pages, and seek out the spirit that inspired them...you will not be disappointed.

Steve Hartlaub has a way with words. He presents the Gospel in a way that you've probably never heard it before. Stripping away all of man's traditions and religion, Steve's writing style is both disarming and refreshing. He makes you take a good, hard look at what you believe and why. Steve backs every study in this book with Holy scripture, digging into the Greek and Aramaic languages to shine a light on the author's intended meaning. Steve encourages you to study the Bible yourself, to see if what he is saying is really true! Dig into the scriptures with this book and let the Holy Spirit guide you and teach you the deeper things of God; namely, the Mystery of Christ! God bless and enjoy your journey with Him!

Normally I hate "Christian" books. Most are so far from what God has communicated to us that they are not worth reading. Even the really good ones have 2 or 3 glaring departures from God's Word. Steve Hartlaub's book is extraordinary. I am just now finishing my second reading. The book makes several critical issues easy to understand. Among them are:

[1] Any understanding of God and His Word comes from God teaching you directly by His Spirit.

[2] The life of faith is resting in what God has already finished through Jesus Christ. Religion always demands us to do something; any version of law is human works, not Christ living through you.

[3] Steve uses the Tree of the Knowledge of Good and Evil to help us understand whether things in life are from God or from the enemy.

If you are only going to read one book, this is the one.

I have known Steve for many years and was delighted to hear the news that he had written the book, **Give me Christ/ Revelations of the Glorified Christ.** He has always been one who has bravely and lovingly learned, lived and taught God's Will by means of Jesus Christ. He is a Gift, his ministry is beautifully manifested in part with the printing of this book. The format is inspirational. The chapters can be likened to taking small steps in a sublime land of milk and honey; each a quick yet fully enriching read. Easy to share and discuss with others I make sure my copy is always near!